NAOMI MITCHISON's
VIENNA DIARY

Vienna Diary
1934

Naomi Mitchison

Kennedy & Boyd

Kennedy & Boyd
an imprint of
Zeticula
57 St Vincent Crescent
Glasgow
G3 8NQ
Scotland

http://www.kennedyandboyd.co.uk
admin@kennedyandboyd.co.uk

First published as *Naomi Mitchison's Vienna Diary*
in 1934 by Victor Gollancz.
This edition Copyright © Estate of Naomi Mitchison
2009

ISBN-13 978 1 84921 021 8
ISBN-10   1 84921 021 7

DEN UNBESIEGTEN GENOSSEN
IN SOLIDARISCHER LIEBE

FOREWORD

FOR REASONS which will become plain in the course of the book, I have, in general, altered names and occasionally cut something out altogether. But otherwise, except for the altering of a word here and there, it is exactly as I wrote it, usually within twelve hours of the events described.

FEBRUARY 23RD : LONDON

Now, I suppose, it really is fixed up. Tickets passport, international driving permit—all that. Have arranged with Coutts's to buy block Schillings in Vienna. An envelope full of introductions. But I am keeping folded up in my bag notes about the people ; this seems safe enough. I don't quite know what clothes to take—anyhow one tidy day dress, and something that will do for semi-evening. It all seems rather improbable.

I didn't know for certain till yesterday evening. Everyone was a bit doubtful ; the woman who had been going with me developed doubts, on the score of probable trouble over the week-end, or next week, and the fact that one might be a nuisance. Finally, she's not coming, and no one else is travelling the same day as me. M. is coming later. I think I rather like the idea of going by myself, but I'm not sure. Let's see what data there are.

Sam definitely wants me to come over. I rang him up last night—it was funny telephoning right across Europe, and the voice at the other end as clear as though it came from Bloomsbury ; it made one's ordinary Newtonian space-time ideas shrivel a little and go unreal. We spoke in terms of a holiday. He seemed very sure that he wanted me over, but said he hoped I was prepared to rough it. I wonder what that means? I wonder what he wants me to do? I hope not anything complicated and illegal, as I am a bad liar. Anyway, that's that, to start with. Now, what about me?

Very few people have both money and leisure—and the will—to do this. I've got this because of my profession. I rang up V. G. on Monday evening, and asked if he'd give me an advance on a—very hypothetical—book about it. He said he would, and I'm going on that. I couldn't have otherwise. Simply as an observer I shall be some use; it's the one thing I'm sure I can do well, though I don't think I'm a good analyser. What I should like to do is to write a full diary every day, as truthful as it can possibly be. I shall type it on both sides of the sheet, so that it will fold small, and shall try and leave a duplicate with somebody—if I get my copy through, they can destroy theirs. But perhaps the whole thing is moonshine; perhaps there won't be anything to write down! If so, looking back on this afternoon from whenever it is in the future, I shall see myself looking a perfect fool. However, that won't be the first time! Anyway, for what it's worth. I feel all thrilled now, screwed up like a child going to play Indians. Perhaps I shall be more grown-up by the end of it.

Well, then, I'm an observer. I'm also a Socialist, and my observations will be the observations of a Socialist, just as they'll be the observations of a

woman of thirty-six, of someone brought up before
the war, partly scientist, partly historian, nothing
complete, the usual set of odds and ends that my
social class and circumstance are likely to produce.
So I shan't be objective. But, then, nobody is, so
that doesn't matter. What other qualifications ?
Bad German, likely to break down at any moment ;
a very limited vocabulary. Anyway I'm bad at
foreign languages. French, fair. I shouldn't be hope-
less at actual relief work, as I had my V.A.D.
training during the war, and am fairly practical at
rolling bandages, and all that. But is there going to
be anything of that sort ?

I'm not brave, and I'm not cool in emergencies.
Probably I'm a sufficient coward to run indoors if I
hear machine guns, otherwise I'm silly enough to
want to look on. I'm bad at making up my mind,
and bad at organising. I get easily excited. Also, I
get easily worried. I'm used to comfort, though I
don't think I mind a reasonable amount of dis-
comfort, so long as I get a decent ration of sleep.
But, when I worry, I don't sleep well.

That's all minus, as far as value goes. Plus, I've
probably got a certain snob-value. I'd make a good
headline if I got imprisoned—probably. Unless
Simon said I wasn't to . . . I might be useful at
impressing people ; I take it one may conceivably
be used to tell whoever happens to be in power that
the attitude of England is this or that. My name's
still some use. I don't suppose I've been definitely

ticked off as a left-winger. And I'm fairly good at
dealing with people, though I don't like it much.
I may look odd, but at least I look fairly distinguished. And I can easily feel like an aristocrat,
which is what makes one behave like one !

The personal factor ? Why am I going—me myself ? A lot of reasons. Partly because I'm really
rather frightened—at moments, very frightened.
I was when my friend at the F.O. told me there was
probably going to be a European war next week.
Now I tell myself that's only F.O. talk. I'm frightened of being hurt—I'm easily hurt—and horribly
frightened of being killed, now, while I'm still at
the height of my power. I've got a bit of a complex
about revolutions ; I feel apocalyptic about them
sometimes—and always frightened. But I know by
experience that the things I'm frightened of hardly
ever turn out to be as bad as I think they'll be
(except, always, child-birth), so if I go now, and it
isn't as bad as I imagine, then I shall cease to feel
towards the idea of revolution as I feel now : terribly
frightened and yet attracted. I expect a good many
people feel that ; they get more and more screwed
up with the effort to prepare for the future, and that
makes them all the less capable of dealing with it
when it comes. I want to get sane about that, and
perhaps the only way is to see for oneself. Then, if
ever the time comes here, I shall be able to be cool
and sensible, and some use. I am often frightened
of things—I was frightened, a little, going to Russia,

which was very silly of me ; and frightened when I went off, alone, to the Crimea—where I enjoyed myself very much. I've been frightened in Morocco, and at sea, and in all sorts of places, but it usually cures one of one sort of terror before one's finished. I hope this will.

I'm lazy, too, and I don't like leaving the children, especially Valentine, who is so delicious now ; and I don't like leaving Dick, and the warm, familiar house, and the smell of pot hyacinths. On the other hand, by going away, I shall get gloriously out of a number of obligations : speeches to make ; letters to write ; people to see ; cocktail parties that I'm too lazy not to go to ; and all the bothering little things —all the things, that keep one's mind switching about like a cow's tail in fly-time; all the things that women are brought up to think about, and that we can't stop thinking about even when we know how silly it is. There are such lots of things one needn't bother about, but one does : household chores, and politenesses in general, and personal relationships. Yes, they do matter in a way, but if one lets one's mind get pulled about from one thing to another, the way mine normally is, one ends by not being able to think at all. I can hardly read a serious book, or follow a serious argument, because my mind is always switching off on to something extraneous and probably trivial. Going to Vienna, I get rid of a lot of that. I shall be able to think, at any rate, about only one kind of thing. It will be a rest and a holiday in a way that ordinary holidays with the children, for instance, never are. I believe this is typical of the she-psychology of this particular place and epoch.

And again, there's ordinary curiosity and sense of adventure. I didn't get much of that as an adolescent, with the war cutting across and limiting everything, and then, when it was over, finding oneself at once a settled householder. People of my age didn't get their fair share of that, and they want to get what they ought to have had younger. Of course, lots of women—almost all women—never do get their fair share of adventure, and they're conditioned not to want it, or—worse—to think that their only sort of adventure can be amorous adventure. That's bad. The difficulty is, we're still not quite equipped for the other sort of adventure (and in trying to equip ourselves, we risk becoming incompetent in the amorous adventures) ; we still can't do just the same things as men ; we still feel we need a certain amount of protection and special treatment. Over this particular adventure, that may be all to the good. A woman may be able to do things which would land a man into trouble. One can often get out of difficulties by being sweetly silly. But I *am* silly over practical things, all the same ; I haven't ever lost my passport yet, but I'm always afraid I may. One is, of course, hampered by inadequate pockets, above all by the fact that one changes one's clothes much oftener than a man !

I think I'm really writing to comfort myself, to fill up time now that I've made all arrangements—I've still got to pack. When I get back it will seem pretty silly, especially when I catch myself thinking, "*If* I get back." But, if one's in my job, one's got to get the stuff out of one somehow. One wants it to be recorded and set down, so that A and B and C—the people who, for one reason or another, matter to one—may know ; so that one won't be alone. I suppose it's a form of our Western hankering for immortality. I keep on wanting to ring people up and tell them I'm going ; I want to be in a group of some sort. It would be much more sensible to try and learn some irregular verbs. I think Dick would do that ; he is being incredibly nice to me about all this, because it's always worst to be the one who's left at home. It would be fun if we were going together. Yet probably it's better for me to be going alone. Or is that Calvinist ? I suppose a man who's a real Socialist feels it extremely important to be—at least over anything serious—a comrade, and not in any way an owner, to his woman. It's probably a quite essential attitude just now ; it's needed to get the women out of their age-old habit of being owned. If he'd said, " No, you mustn't," I would have been very cross, but some inside part of me would have been disgustingly, ancestrally satisfied. And, by just that tiny bit, the spirit of the future, of mankind, would have been delayed. At least, that's my theory of it. If he and I didn't like living together as much as we do,

15

there'd be no value in going away from one another. Or is this Calvinist again ? Anyhow, it makes one value the living together. I thought that this morning, all the time between waking and his going off to work, just this easy business of seeing one another, going in and out of rooms, dressing and hair-brushing, Valentine trotting about—one only knows what it is when something happens to put it in focus, make one set value by it. Otherwise it's just too easy. Perhaps that's the difficulty of marriage— once people have become conscious enough to think about it at all.

Now it's about tea-time, and Lois is back from school, and, in a minute, she or Avrion will come in and tell me tea's ready, and there it'll all be, for to-day. And when will it be again ? I don't know, and I must stop writing or I shall just begin to dither.

. . . .

Why, when one's nervous, does one either eat nothing or much more than usual ? Eating is very much bound up with the nerve centres. But now Angela has rung up, to tell me of several people who've started already—what the hell is there to be nervous about, anyway ? I suppose one gets like this through regarding oneself, not one's job ; they will have been thinking of their job—and other people.

I'm rather glad to be missing the hunger-marchers on Sunday ; I'd meant to go and look on, and I feel that Hyde Park will be just one galaxy of highbrows, all out for Justice and Free Speech. And we'd meet and gabble. I'm not going to take any modern highbrow books. I've taken Southey's *The Doctor*, which looks good and remote, but I shall try and read some German newspapers. Avrion and Valentine have been playing at sabre-tooth tigers—every now and then Valentine lost her nerve, shouted, " I don't want to be etten," and rushed back to me to be picked up. They both have this grand feeling of confidence in the universe, and at the same time that nothing matters—they're gay. I wonder how long they'll be able to keep that ?

FEBRUARY 24TH

Now at last I'm off. The train is passing through fogged Kentish hop-fields. Dick will be on his way, north-west from London, for King's Norton. The hunger-marchers are walking in towards their centre. There should be a good row to-morrow, now that the fools have arrested Pollitt and Tom Mann.

Yesterday evening, letters and telephone calls. Goodness knows when the main Fund will get out. M. rang up, rather dispirited about it ; they'd had no report from Vienna. The Save the Children

Fund people are depressed too, and doubt if they'll
get much money. The Friends will hold a committee
meeting next week. In view of that, and the letters,
I'm glad I'm taking some money out. I have about
£30 in English money, and nearly £10 in Austrian.
Another £100 going out. At the station, H. met us,
and said he'd asked his bank to send me out £25.
I was awfully pleased—and pleased to see him too.
I shall have to behave sensibly and come back safe,
just to show him that he and all the Haldanes are
wrong ! I gave him a specimen signature for his
bank, just as the train started, which seemed, somehow, very cinema-ish. And Dick will have to sign
all the household cheques for next month ! Margaret
says I'm running away—so I am, partly. So'd she if
she had my particular chance, and wasn't committed
with things up to the eyes. So would a lot of women.
I'm sure half the people who say they disapprove
are really envious !

I think of all the people I've met and telephoned
to this week ; of Maisky at the Embassy party,
smiling and being nicely mysterious, as though
everything were going to be all right—he always
makes one feel that, much as a religious person does,
but not annoyingly. He has a sense of happy destiny.
Of other people at the party—Ellen Wilkinson and
Dorothy Woodman, the bad girls of the Labour
movement, always playing with the naughty boys
and getting away with it ; Margaret, dark and fierce
and smiling, telling one what she thinks of people

several seconds before they're out of hearing ; Susan Lawrence giving one an impression of complete efficiency (does she ever miss trains or lose her bag ?) ; the nice but comic Russian educationist telling me stories of the ideologic Russian children teaching their grandmothers to suck eggs ; Johnny Pritt, Ray, Mrs. Burton. Of the various people who've been discouraging, too, either on the lines that one wasn't wanted or that one oughtn't to go taking risks, that, in fact, one was merely being childish.

Now we're at Dover ; I'm writing on the boat. When I was really a child we stayed here one summer, and I used to watch the ships and feel very romantic about them, in a Kiplingish way. Funny, living on an island. I suppose I was thirteen that summer when I got out of it for the first time ; I never travelled alone, even on the island, till I was sixteen. It was the custom. We skirt along the island, along the greyish white of the cliffs, till they double back into the light fog and we begin to lose them. I don't think I should ever be really lonely so long as I have my typewriter ; it is part of me, part of my working self, but sufficiently apart to be companionable—like a doll, I suppose. It has certain tricks and mannerisms, irritating perhaps, but so much itself that I don't bother to get them put right. When I was in Russia, they used to give me a room to myself because of it—my *malenkay mashina*—but nobody else respects machines as much as that. The things I had in Russia are all rather part of me, the

19

little solid-fuel saucepan—my *malenky samovar*—I've brought it with me, and some tea. One doesn't get much attached to a suitcase, but one does to a rucksack. Rucksack and typewriter and suitcase are really too heavy to carry, but I can just manage them. They may be lighter coming back.

IN THE TRAIN: FEBRUARY 25TH

There is, then, the moment when the ship turns heavily, backing into its own tossed and greyish wake. And we, strapping ourselves about with heavy weights, straining our arms with heavy English or German cases, stare at the dull quays as though really they held something necessary to our fog-damped spirits. So, still expectant, we pass customs, and emerge on low Continental platforms, looking at train boards covered with holiday names—names of Easter or Whitsun trips as advertised. Or beyond, to Istanbul, Bucarest, Beograd, romantic names still more heavily romanticised in Mitropean spelling and ugly type. And so one settles into the carriage which is to be one's small and squarish home during almost thirty hours.

The afternoon was still and not cold, and devastat-ingly grey. Since the train was to stand here another hour, I walked out of the station with feminine English timidity, and so into the town, where all the shops appeared to be shut, not even a café to give one a first taste of foreign life. At the corner of a street, a woman and I approached one another, hesitating, each recognising a fellow-passenger from the boat, and the one whose luggage also lay in the compartment to Vienna. She was pretty, in a coat of softly shaded leopard skin, and a close brown hat ; hair chestnut and wavy under the hat brim ; delicate eyebrows, perhaps plucked ; complexion pale to warm ; high cheek-bones ; a sapphire and diamond ring. She spoke to me in German, then, at my halting reply, in goodish English. We walked together, towards what in summer would have been the fashionable sea-front. At first we were suspicious, conversationally smelling round one another, then each beginning to suspect the other of good intentions. She, I find, is Viennese, with one child—and a divorced husband—in Vienna. We speak tentatively of the troubles ; she says why did they fight against the Government when all it meant was that they would be killed ? What is the use of dead men ? I say, but—— I talk a little of why I am going and my own convictions. At that, a little less cautious, she counters that she is a Jewess—I had not particularly noticed or thought of that. We begin to talk more freely. It seems possible that there is a definite humanitarian instinct among the Spanish Jews—she speaks bitterly of all politics, especially of the two interests which are squeezing her country, for she feels Austrian, though now, she says, for the child's sake she must go. She has, I suppose, the real Liberal mentality, with great sympathy for all the decencies of practical democracy ; for the crèches and kindergartens now blown to bits, most of all. Her own family has had troubles, caught up in war and civil war, always holding to some practical internationalism.

Back in the train, which now drew out towards Bruges, I realised that I should not be lonely this journey, nor even for that matter sufficiently alone for the various vague idea forms in my mind to settle and crystallise. I realised, too, how one is always unwilling to face being alone with one's ideas—how one prefers the easy contacts of civilised minds—and I wondered what I should make of a spell of prison. We went on talking ; she offered me an orange, whose smell led me to talk of Christmas-trees and ask her if she had one. But she said no, she could not give her child that while Jews were still being persecuted by Christians. She spoke of the present state of affairs in Vienna, the anti-Semitism, which seems on the whole unreal, rather ludicrous, to us, but which was plainly and horribly real to her and her friends. All the Jews there seem prepared for the thing to happen as in Germany—they are waiting to be turned out ; doctors or lawyers in the meantime finding their practices dwindling—professors learning poultry farming. Do we in England and Scotland not feel anti-Semite simply because we

22

are sufficiently intelligent ourselves to be able to enter our own learned professions, so that there is no racial jealousy ? And are our anti-Semites simply the people who are too stupid to pass exams, get professorships, and so on, themselves ? Or, if we were oppressed from outside into unhappiness and inferiority and hate, would we, too, look for a scapegoat and find the same one ?

In the over-heated carriage, both she and I grew sleepy, and slept on and off during the evening. It is annoying how in this state of half sleep, with the barriers down, things get at one which one is normally guarded against—one's own and other people's stupidities and unkindnesses, tear-making. But if one shakes them off, coming on guard again, the mere fact that one is defended stops sleep from coming. For a time I read the Berlitz grammar, and tried to memorise irregular verbs.

Then came the German frontier. My companion was agitated, I not, still secure with my British passport which made me spiritual heir of all the milords who have in the grand commercial past swaggered over the Continent. There was no trouble ; my companion even said that she had never found them so polite. Warned by her, I had earlier torn out a good article on Austria from *Time and Tide*. They asked if we had papers, confiscated a Belgian one, left the *Daily Telegraph*, and, after looking at it rather uncomprehendingly, left *Time and Tide*. They then searched under the seats with a flash-lamp,

very seriously and solemnly. But did not find
so much as a Communist. My poor companion was
really unhappy at getting into Germany—would
have gone round by Paris, only this was the quicker
way to get to the child—but at last slept, and so
did I.

Next morning we woke to dullish country, which
later turned to small hills and terraced vines. I
stared out at the towns, and there sure enough were
the swastika flags, red and black and white, slung
magnificently from newly painted poles or dangled
out of windows. There were some of the old Imperial
striped flags too, and, as we got into Bavaria, a few
blue and white ones. It seemed a little difficult to
take these very gaudy flags quite seriously ; they
were so very like children's-party decorations, stuck
about in the same kind of way. Sometimes we passed
a place where wild land had been newly taken into
cultivation for vines, and here one little wild tree
was always left, but hung with strips of bright-
coloured paper ; that seemed, somehow, realer and
more permanent than the flags.

The people at the stations looked much the same,
rather nice, rather stupid, badly dressed, no political
evidence. Würzburg, where the Brygos kylix is, and
Nürnberg, which is connected with all our child-
hoods, were hung with flags, especially little ones
sticking out of the windows of workers' flats. My
companion told me horrid stories of mediæval
cruelties practised here during the terror. There is

snow, half melted, everywhere, and pine-trees, pretty enough. Everything looks ridiculously normal All my London timidities now seem quite idiotic.

We have just discovered that this flag-day is some kind of war commemoration. One wonders if people are being worked up for the anniversary of the Reichstag fire—or whatever else may be going to happen at the end of the week. Now it is dinner-time. My companion refuses to eat until she is in Austria, but I take a dining-car ticket, which later I regret, for the food is less good and more expensive than it would be in France or even England. We see some evidence of militarism at the stations—soldiers, some wearing swastika arm-bands, and camouflaged waggons loaded on trucks. My companion has some interesting criticism of England ; she says the girls are stupid, neither intellectual nor housewives, and she is—how rightly !—shocked by our extravagances. She had been taken to dine at a big hotel, and the meal cost about £2 per head. I don't suppose that's anything like what London meals can be if they try, but it certainly is very shocking when one comes to think of it.

At the Austrian frontier, less fuss about customs and so on, and friendlier people. We cease, thank goodness, to see swastikas, but instead see the blue cornflower of the Austrian Nazi Party, adopted when the swastika was forbidden, and now, in its turn, forbidden too—but sometimes worn. On the whole, people have nicer faces ; you don't see these

incredibly brutal faces that crop up in Germany—
the *Bahn-polizei* man at one of the Bavarian places
looked as if he'd happily shoot one at sight—not that
one can always trust in looks. I bought a *Wiener
Freie Presse*, but there seemed to be no news in it—
except that Pollitt and Mann are out on bail. It has
to fill itself up with odd bits about murders in
Chicago—even the Loch Ness monster came in !

Just beyond Passau the country is as good as it can
well be. After the north European fogs, there's now
brilliant sunshine, beating in warm, drawing up
young crops, though here and there are still patches
of bright snow. The Donau Valley is lovely and full
of colours—soft blues and browns—though the river
is low, not covering the stones at the sides. I wonder
what people in the Middle Ages would have said
to this drought all over Europe ? Whose fault is it ?

FEBRUARY 26TH : VIENNA

I want to try and get my impressions into order.
The train came in an hour late, after delay at Linz,
through beautiful country, moonlit thin snow (I
said it was like a Breughel landscape, and my companion said, " How different you are from other
English women ! " But, as I explained, I know

26

nothing about tennis. . . .) Sam met me, and drove to the hotel, while I told him firmly all the things I would in no circumstances do. He then explained things, and later I went down and saw two of the others, who confirmed, in a slightly comic con-spiratorial atmosphere of talking in whispers—no doubt quite necessary.

As I had supposed, even in England, the Dollfuss "relief" is being used for Catholic and "Patriotic Front" propaganda. Naturally, they don't want any other relief, and will, in general, sabotage it. There seem to be one or two minor "actions" which are really helpful, especially one for getting children away, but, in general, little can be done officially by outside organisations. That means that most relief work must be done through the Social Demo-crats themselves, who are actually doing it with whatever money they can get. They have their own doctors and nurses, and, of course, almost all the victims are on their side—others will certainly be well looked after by the Dollfuss "relief." Naturally, their people can't just go respectably to hospital, as they would be hanged, or imprisoned, when well enough to come out.

That is to say that most of the funds must be administered direct by the people actually involved. Some can be done through the Friends (who are already dealing with a few obvious neutral bad cases—old people and so on), and perhaps the Save the Children Fund, so that any non-Socialists who

27

have contributed to the English relief fund can be certain that their money is being distributed through neutral channels. But, in general, it is important that the main amount should go straight *from comrades to comrades*. It is not charity, it is international solidarity and love. That must be understood.

Again : the Social Democratic Party is not dead. It is very much alive, though, of course, driven underground. There are still good people left, and it is our job, as Socialists, to help. There are several ways of doing this. I understand that I can be used in one way. One may even be saving the lives of fine and valuable people—the type which civilisation can ill spare. As a humanitarian, and as some one with a scientific outlook, my course seems clear.

Again : it is very necessary to get news of what is happening here into England, and of getting English news—the news of what English public opinion is about—into Austria. As to getting news out : it's one thing getting the facts into England, but it's another getting them published. From Vienna, Sam sees it all as urgent and vital, and, above all, desperately interesting. But, as I told him, Austria is not really news in England any longer. What with Maundy Gregory and the drought, and all the film stars in the world, people don't want to read about Austria ; and the newspapers are, as we all know, the servants of the people. Equally, it is only some of the newspapers who would put the stuff in, even if it were news. A large part of the Press would, of course, suppress it.

As to the future. There is likely to be a Nazi show of some sort at the end of the week. As one had supposed, many of the workers are going Nazi, just because they will then get weapons and be able to get back on the Government. If you want revenge badly enough, you won't bother about selling your soul to get it. Dear little Dollfuss, whom everyone in England feels all motherly about, appears to be extremely well hated. If the situation remains as it is, the Nazis are likely to win. They appear to have a number of key positions. Against them are Italian opinion, money, and, conceivably, force ; also French opinion and, perhaps, money. If England were against them too, things would be different. It seems like a case for using the League to save (or neutralise) Austria. This might be a test case for making or breaking the League. If the workers saw a chance of this happening, they would probably not join the Nazis, but would stick to their own show. After all, they are the majority here in Vienna, and they still have some power. But, with Simon's present attitude, it seems unlikely that anything of the sort will happen.

Even if the Nazis win, that does not kill Social Democracy in Austria ; it is too deep. But it is impossible at the moment to say what will happen. No doubt I shall become clearer in a day or two about the actual political situation. Certain things

about the immediate past are clear. The Social
Democrats were not betrayed by their leaders,
although no doubt occasions have been misjudged.
The whole thing was precipitated by the Linz affair,
and the general strike, even, was hardly organised.
But the usual Communist Party allegations are
ill-founded and in bad taste. The Social Democratic
Party was extremely wide ; all wings had collabor-
ated ; it was as united a front as anyone could ask
for. Whether a different policy should have been
adopted fifteen years ago is mainly of academic
interest now.

I take it that things were much more nearly
touch and go during the fighting than we supposed
in England. The Social Democrats were more fully
armed than we realise. It seems clear that humanitarian motives definitely stopped them from using
all their arms. But humanitarian motives did not
stop the Government from shelling them. Whether
this is inevitable in any struggle between Socialists
and reactionaries, is a question for the historian. I
think myself that Socialism, being based on love and
equality, *must* be humanitarian, even though it may
mean that in its beginnings it has to be defeated. As,
for the time, it has been defeated here. As, here, it
has lost nearly 500 dead in Vienna alone—and will
lose more from among the prisoners if nothing is
done to save them.

The other factor which made the issue uncertain
was that there is no complete accord between Fey

and Dollfuss. Anything might have happened. No doubt Dollfuss tried to compromise ; no doubt he is doing so still, and will. We in England supposed that the workers could not possibly, in modern conditions and with modern armaments, win. From what Sam tells me, this was not so. At present I am still uncertain what, during the next few days, and in the future, supposing the Nazi coup is averted or—more likely—compromised with, the Social Democrats can do. It is at any rate clear that they must have the moral and practical support of the Socialists of other countries, especially of England (I feel, perhaps wrongly, that the Austrian and the English parties contain much the same type of person, especially a large mass of skilled and decent workers, and a number of brave idealists). We have to help to restore their morale. We have to make it worth while for humanity—for the great pattern and music of the future—that their men and women should have died ; that many should still be in immediate jeopardy of death ; that many should now be in the utmost pain of body and mind.

I do not know for certain how I can help. I can write things down clearly and truthfully, and I will do so. I promise now that this diary will contain nothing but the truth. It will not be the whole truth, partly because no man or woman can ever know that, and partly because I shall probably be unable to say certain things, so as not to endanger other people. I will do nothing which my conscience, as a lover of mankind and as a practical woman, forbids me to do.

It is very curious, but a number of people in England, and perhaps even some in Scotland, look on me as a wild revolutionary. This only shows how easily people can be misled. Because sections of Church opinion have quarrelled with me, I haven't stopped trying to live up to the main ideas of Jesus, although my intellect forbids me to accept the later superstructure. But a lot of people think I am a bad and dangerous woman. Thus anything which I sign myself is suspect to those people. I wish they would realise that one who, like myself, has lived all her life with the outlook of a scientist and historian, is obviously going to be no good as a propagandist.

Before writing any more, I am going to look round, and present some of my introductions.

Towards mid-day I went off into the town. Externally it seems cheerful enough, though not rich—there isn't a tenth of the London or Paris traffic, very few private cars. Prices seem low. There was little hurry or argument in the streets. Several times I passed detachments of soldiers of some kind, mostly Heimwehr, often thin and stupid-looking, with untidy-looking trousers and feathers in their hats, or else in steel helmets. All had rifles, and the police seem to have revolvers and large swords, and truncheons as well. There were advertisements of the Heimwehr—the " Save Your Country " business—also advertisements of the official relief works.

I called on G,, but didn't find him, then on Lass, who was in, but asked me to come back later. Then I went to see the Friends—found people, mostly very poor and ragged looking, queued up for some soup kitchen by a church. Beggars about in every street. Had lunch at a small restaurant. I'm still ridiculously shy about having meals by myself, with a sort of Calvinist complex about ordering the things I like least ! I came back to the Friends, and found E. C. there ; later H. C. came in. They are both rather formidable. The Friends are naturally very anxious to be completely non-political, and are preserving this attitude so successfully that it seems a little doubtful whether they will be able to do anything at all. Of course I am in no position to judge, but I couldn't help feeling that they might possibly be turning a slightly blind eye on what is happening. At any rate, there is nothing much for me to do there.

Came back to Lass, who was full of stuff. She is no party politician—laughed at it all, rather, from the position of the intellectual and artist. But she has seen a lot. She says there is frightful difficulty in getting anyone to accept money or help—suspicion everywhere ; no one will admit to being Socialists, or even in need. However, she has contacts, and promises to take me, to-morrow, to see people. She was tremendously impressed by the general decency of the men and women who have suffered, and what a fine show the Gemeinde Hauser were.

Like everyone else, she hadn't a word for Dollfuss, and can't understand the ordinary English point of view about his being a nice little man. She has the same story of the workers going over to the Nazis, and seems to think a coup not unlikely, though her Nazi acquaintances emphasise that they want peace. She also told me of the Czech aeroplanes that came over during the fighting and scattered leaflets to encourage the workers—which were, however, almost all blown away, and the rest rapidly collected by the authorities.

Came back to Sam's. Several people there, including Z, to whom I was handed over. I walked, with Z, across the town to see Y. Z explained things from her point of view ; she is apparently less hopeful than Sam. She says the party (in which she has been all her life) is smashed, though many of the workers hardly realise it, because they have become so much accustomed to take it for granted—it provided so much more than politics : amenities ; housing ; clubs ; all the type of things like sickness and unemployment benefit. They don't realise yet that it's gone. But they will. She says that the only hope, and it is a small one, is to get in some kind of moderate Government (best, the " Christian Socialists "—minus Dollfuss, whom his own original party don't think too well of now) which will allow them to pick themselves up ; which will, at any rate, not kill them all or put them into concentration camps. The alternatives are Austrian Nazis, the Heimwehr—probably having shed Dollfuss—or the German Nazis. She had even a little good to say of the German Nazis, compared with their own. She trotted across the town with me, explaining all this, past flower-sellers with Christmas-roses and snowdrops and mimosa ; she seemed wonderfully cheerful, considering that she was waiting to be arrested any moment.

We came to Y's office. He peered out, past a chained door, then he let us in, and drew Z aside to whisper to her, I tactfully standing back. Then we were taken through to an inner room ; Y probably trusted me, in so far as anyone trusts anyone they don't know personally and absolutely, but he was not, and could not be, helpful. One could see his morale was badly shattered ; he sat in a chair slackly, his hands loose at the wrists, peering and frowning. Z made suggestions ; he did not accept them. I made suggestions ; nothing seemed much good. He did not know how to get in touch with people—so-and-so was never at home now ; so-and-so could not be telephoned to or written to. Everything had broken down. Many of his friends had been killed, others were in danger. No doubt it is so for thousands of men and women ; I got a desperate impression of broken morale. A meeting was arranged for later on ; he would write down nothing —it was better never to write. By now it had got dusk ; I said, " At least, let us know one another again." He seemed reluctant even to turn on the light.

35

We came back, through the defeated city, to Sam's. More talk. I am beginning to wonder how the money will be distributed when it comes. It seems as if a few people—mostly, perhaps, outsiders—must arrange it, building up right from tne beginning. Sam wants me to write an article, which I am doing with some reluctance, especially as the stuff is not to my mind what will go over in England. I won't sign it, as it is not first hand. I keep on emphasising— I did to Y and Z—that I must see things *for myself*. But I am still uncertain how to do it.

I had a longish talk to one of the less official correspondents, a nice man, who agrees with my point about keeping out of the news. But even he, having been through the fighting and seen some pretty beastly things with his own eyes, doesn't realise how little Austria is news now in England. When he talks of atrocities, I keep on thinking how apt one is to skip atrocity stories (after all, one must live, and such stories, if one begins to allow the imagination to vivify them, are shattering), how one says, " Oh, it's only the *Manchester Guardian* again." Probably, when I've been out here a bit longer, I shall get the point of view that things must be put across, and shall bore all my friends in England by talking about it, when I get back.

I hear talk of the Floridsdorf police-station, and men beaten to death there. Everyone—here and abroad—said that the Austrians would never be as beastly and brutal as the Germans. And so *we* say

about the possibilities of Fascism in England. It is
the kind of lie one can't help believing, for it goes so
well with one's inclinations. As it is there has been a
good deal of Dollfuss-clemency-stuff put across. It
seems reminiscent of the notorious clemencies of
J. Cæsar.

FEBRUARY 27TH : AFTERNOON

Yesterday evening I telephoned to Dick, who had
little news—and it was, in a way, unpleasant to be so
apparently near and yet unable even to speak
plainly of urgent things for fear of overhearing.
Dined with Sam and one of those nice, ordinary,
spectacled little Americans who seem to spring up in
any foreign country and be willing to do the oddest
errands ; he looks gloriously un-suspect. After dinner
got the rest of the Wallisch stuff and wrote the article
which, with my letter, went off to-day to Laski, not,
of course, by the ordinary post. Also wrote to Dick,
enclosing earlier diary and some pretty horrible
stuff about prisons and so on, including what had
happened at the Floridsdorf police-station. It was
then very late, and I had to get up early to go off
with Lass. We changed another £5—I had already
given her £10—and went off. On my way to her I

had seen a kind of parade of Heimwehr all along a street. People stood and looked at them, without much expression.

Lass had a long list of people. She had the first names from the teachers at the Gemeinde Model Kindergarten where her small boy goes : there were no children there whose parents had been in trouble, but the teachers had friends or relations teaching at State schools in the shelled areas . . . and so the names turned up. The teachers were not at all anxious to keep the names in their possession— anything written may be dangerous—but they passed on scribbled lists of the bad cases. And in the last couple of days she has had lists from other people, some of whom she knows, others whom she doesn't. She took a few names to the Friends, but there was nothing doing. They said they had no money. It was interesting to contrast this with *The Times*, which says that Mrs. Dollfuss is looking so nicely after everyone.

There is, apparently (but everything is rumour in Vienna) a certain amount of money from Czecho-Slovakia which is being used for relief work ; it is of course the only near-by State which sympathises with the workers. But otherwise—— However, to go on with the morning : looking at the lists, one was struck by the large number of Hungarian and perhaps Czech names. Usually there was some kind of note on the case ; very few families had more than two or three children. Lass told me that was confirmed later, that the *Hauswarte* (the porters for each staircase, who had probably always been particularly respectable party men) in each of the Gemeinde Hauser were being turned out and replaced by spies.

We got a bus at the Stephans-Platz, the middle of tourist Vienna, with its two-star cathedral and a restaurant where I remember having a very good dinner the last time I was in Vienna—nine years ago. It bumped us mercilessly over cobbles, over the Donau Canal, and into a definitely non-tourist district—little shops, tenements, waste ground, factories, one fine-looking Gemeinde Haus : beyond were the gas-works where, during the fighting, a handful of men kept the Heimwehr at bay, threatening to blow up the city, and were only at last induced to surrender by the lie that all the other districts had already surrendered. Beyond that, the mountains, near and beautiful. So across the Donau itself, and almost immediately came signs of fighting—odd-looking chips and holes, one distant block with very distinct shell-holes. We got off at the terminus ; here all the plaster was chipped with bullet-marks, and people's faces looked different from in the centre. Lass told me that when she first came out all the glass was still broken, and all the tram wires beyond here were down. But it had all been cleared up very quickly. However, people's feelings cannot be cleared up or mended as quickly as that.

We went to our first case, in an oldish tenement block behind shops. An old woman, with lumps on

39

her face, half opened the door. " Don't be afraid,"
said Lass, " we are English ; we are strangers ; we
have come to see if you need help " ; and repeated
again : " Haben Sie nicht Angst." It was like that at
every door we went to where she was not known
already. At last the old woman opened the door and
let us in, and she and a young woman stared at us
with fear and suspicion still very near. It was a small
kitchen ; there was one child. Lass gave the younger
woman twenty Schillings (this was the usual sum
we gave everyone) ; she took it doubtfully. And then
the older woman burst into tears and began sobbing
about, " Mein Bub', mein Bub' "—her son (the
younger woman's husband) was in prison ; he had
been away fourteen days, there was no news ; I tried
to comfort her ; the tears ran down over the lumps
in her face ; the younger woman still stared, holding
the money.

Then we went on down the main street to the
Schlinger Hof, one of the older of the Gemeinde
Hauser, built in 1925, but fine enough with a rather
Dutch architectural effect, and a sloping tiled roof,
which had been smashed in some places. As we came
close, we found plenty of glass not yet mended, and
all the houses were small-poxed with bullet marks.
But it was the faces which were worst. Everyone
looked as sick as muck. All the mouths were turned
down ; all complexions pale as though from surgical
shock ; no one spoke loud or laughed. They did not
even observe us foreigners. The women looked as if

they'd been in front of the P.A.C. ; there were red eyes and noses, and crumpled handkerchiefs.

We went to the first address, where Lass had been before ; it was two rooms—both large—one a living-kitchen, the other a bedroom with twin beds, good furniture, clean linen. In one bed was a white-faced woman, who caught Lass and kissed her hands, and began talking quickly and nervously. There was a man standing by her, looking pale and queer—a big strong man, but he seemed to have been put through the mangle. He was her husband, just out of prison ; she had five brothers—I think all were now out, but most had been in prison. Her mother came in, talking through tears about new shootings at Linz. She began to dither about her nerves and the effect it had on her stomach. She had been ill when it started. All greeted us—as many did later—with a " Grüss-Gott."

The next family was unusual, a woman with eight children—but a strong, intelligent woman, trying to cope with things. She said, though, that the children's nerves were so bad they didn't dare go to the kinder-garten (in the building itself) because of the police and soldiers, although the police were now trying to make friends with them. They screamed when they went to the lavatory ; they cried and stopped their ears. What I want to explain is that these are a good sort of people, able on the whole to afford a reason-able amount of furniture, bed-linen, and so on—a fair degree of comfort. They are what in England would be called a good class of tenant. They kept the paintwork well ; there was seldom any smell on the common stair ; they had brass plates with their names on the white-painted doors—and always a queer little peep-hole, so that, before they let us in, the shutter at the back of this would move and they would stare at us.

We went across tram-lines, down streets, and over a railway crossing, between these eternal groups of two or three whispering and glancing round, and so to Gartenstadt. Lass had not been here before, but had the names from a friend. This is a most beautiful Gemeinde Haus, high and airy and generous, with balconies and great courtyards, and a view out on to the hills. In front is a half circle of grass and bushes and flower-beds, lilacs in fat bud, and young oak-trees. There were Nazi swastikas painted on it, and half rubbed out—the other house was still flying the white flag ; they are made to do that. We knocked at a door, and a frightened woman opened it. Lass began : " We are from England—strangers— please do not be afraid." But the woman was terrified, and at first would not let us in. Then a neighbour came in, and summed us up and talked to the woman, soothing her. I want to describe this neighbour : she was strong and solid, not very tall, with beautiful golden-brown, wavy hair, blue eyes, and a smiling mouth, very Nordic looking—German perhaps, and yet at once she made me think of King's Norton and the best kind of people there ;

she was the real stuff that Labour Parties are made of. She was young and alive and still hopeful. Perhaps I am feeling romantic about her, but she seemed to me like the spirit of democracy—she was as strong and helpful as the Athenian women who hold up the porch of the Erectheum. Her hands were good to touch. She soothed the older women, then, and we came into the usual clean, gay little house, with many more fresh-laundered curtains, and shining china, than most English homes. At last the woman told us that her nephew was " gone," and his wife and three sons were in prison. She had nothing.

In the next dwelling there was a frightened old woman again, but the neighbour, whom I will call Mrs. T., pulled on a beret, and came with us and explained us to people ; that made each visit take half the time. I was wanting by now to say that the money was English Labour money, but it seemed not very possible. In one flat the people were out, in another there was only a boy, who did not seem willing to take anything. In another, the husband was " gone "—the girl whispered that he was safe in Brünn, *Gott sei dank!* These were mostly two- and three-roomed dwellings, all beautifully light, some with magnificent views ; most of the people had good furniture, and lots of knick-knacks. It was all extraordinarily unsordid, unlike an English " model dwelling." The common stairs were of course enclosed, and very light and pleasant, with well-designed banisters. On each landing were two to four

43

doors, each glossy-white painted, with bright brass
fittings and name-plate. But now most of the doors
showed signs of having been forced ; under the white
paint the wood was torn and splintered.

I decided that I must see Mrs. T. again—she spoke
good German, that I could understand, and
besides—— Well, I liked her, and I think she liked
me. I said I would come back that evening ; and
I said, " Auf Wiedersehen, Genosse," and she
gripped my hand, for a moment, a little harder ; I
had not felt able to say that word before. As it was,
of course I ought to have said *Genossin* ! The last time
anyone had called me *Genossin*, was a German-
speaking Russian girl—an aeroplane engineer—on
the train between Odessa and Kiev ; she, too, had
been fair and thick-set and strong-looking.

We went back to the Schlinger Hof. In the first
house, the woman was sitting at a table, crying
bitterly ; a neighbour opened the door for us. She
took the money, without looking at it ; her husband
was up before the *Stand-gericht* (martial law) ; that
is the worst of all. As we went up and down the
stairs, sometimes doors opened and people peered
out ; once we saw a man with a bare foot, heavily
bandaged round the instep. Lass's leg was very tired
now, and I was foot-sore. The next dwelling was less
tidy than some, but the people were very friendly—
they were the first Lass had seen just after the fighting.
The husband is a tramway-man, there are two or three
children, and the wife is pregnant. It is a two-roomed

flat (the flats always include a w.c., but not a bath-room—each dwelling has good communal bath and wash-house) but the rooms are large and light—there is, of course, electric light and running water, as everywhere, and gas for cooking. On the wall were a dozen little coloured pictures by the child at school ; the man tried to tell me something about them, but he talked such a thick dialect that I could not follow it at all. When Lass first came the hus-band was still at the police-station ; now he is back, and in work, but he is very much afraid he will be turned out. He has been there for ten years, but that won't matter now. Two or three people a day are being given notice, and new hands taken on ; prob-ably these new men will not be Social Democrats but " Christian Socialists " (the bitter way she said the word *Christliche* !), but that isn't all : the original employees were getting sixty-eight Austrian Schillings a week—not a very princely wage, but at least the Gemeinde Haus rents are cheap—whereas the be-ginners are only getting forty-eight. All the trade unions are broken up, and for those who have been in prison the Municipal Pensions Scheme is stopped —they will get nothing for back contributions.

Mrs. H., the wife, offered to go round with us—it was a great help. But she was very careful only to speak in whispers while we were outside on the stair-cases. Already some of the *Hauswarte* (the porters for each stair, who drew a small salary for looking after things, and who were generally party members)

45

have been turned out and been replaced by spies. This will presumably be done in all the Gemeinde Hauser.

At the first address—which Mrs. H. herself told us about—a woman with a sore eye opened the door and let us in ; while Mrs. H. and Lass explained, she leant against the gas-stove and cried a little. Mrs. H. told us how, after the fighting, every single man over eighteen in the whole Schlinger Hof was arrested and taken away, including cripples and those lying sick in bed—the eldest was seventy-two—they got about seven hundred men altogether. They were driven out into the street. I have heard, on the authority of a man who ought to know, that the Heimwehr fired into them from behind. But perhaps I should take the quieter version of these two women—that there was fighting still going on between groups, and the men were shot accidentally. It is at least definite that these prisoners were driven into a place where some would be certain to be killed. At least nine of them were—I have heard larger numbers. Amongst them was Mr. Schmidt. He had at one time been a party member, but his heart has been bad ever since the war, and he had taken no part in politics for some years ; he was a railway-man. Mrs. Schmidt took her husband's registration card out of her bodice, and showed it to us ; we murmured unhappily, not knowing what we could say about this ugly, blonde, stupid-looking man with the big moustache, who had been killed so unnecessarily, and whose

46

wife was crying for him. But Mrs. H., more practical, said : " But I had thought him fatter than that." This cheered the widow up. " No, no," she said, " that was his brother ; that was Johann " ; and then she asked us if we would like to see her bullet-hole. We went through ; it was a three-roomed flat, a big kitchen-living-room, with an embroidered back to the gas-stove and china on the sideboard ; the next room with twin beds of polished wood for her and the blond railway-man who was shot ; and beyond, a small room with a bluebell and violet stencil, where her two little girls sleep. It was early on Wednesday (or possibly Tuesday) morning, and she had just got them up, uncertain what to do, when a bullet came through the window, through the head of her bed, through the little girls' bed, and ended in the chest of drawers. It must have been shot from the house across the road, and from a higher level, as it was pointing downward—I don't think a spent bullet would have gone through a window, two beds, and a plaster wall. Otherwise there was no damage ; she had embroidered covers to the beds, and embroidered linen strips over the lintels of the doors.

As we went, Mrs. H. whispered that the police car had just gone—three men and a woman (I think) had been arrested this time. It is this constant fear of re-arrest which is driving them mad. They never know when the police car may not drive up again. On the stairs, more forced doors. We went to another flat, and several men and women gathered to discuss things. Here the man looked desperately ill ; he had been in prison ; he wouldn't talk to us. We spoke of another couple ; the husband was wounded. We asked if the *Fürsorgerin* was coming to him ; someone answered, " The *Fürsorgerin* does not come ; her husband has been shot." Every man we saw must have been in prison, for a few days anyhow, and after a time we began to realise the point of this. According to one of Dollfuss's new laws, passed only three months ago (just nicely in time), all unemployment pay is stopped if a man has had so much as one day's imprisonment, even in a police-station. Nor is it known when or whether he can get it back. Ordinarily his pay is stopped after he has been unemployed for two years, but often a man will pay ten Schillings to anyone who will employ him for a week, and re-start the two-year period. Now the thousands of unemployed workers who were imprisoned for a few days last week, or the week before, have had their pay stopped and their numbers taken off the official register of numbers. It seems a simple way of economising ; I wonder our own National Government hasn't thought of it ! But perhaps they have.

In another flat there was no answer ; a neighbour came out and whispered to us that the man was in the *Untersuchungs-Gefängnis*, a criminal court where the examinations happen, and the wife had gone to try and see him. It was all so different from how those flats should have been. They had pleasant courtyards, with grass and ornamental bushes ; there were kindergartens and an arcade. But everywhere these dreadful little whispering groups.

We went to try and see the *Fürsorgerin*. A boy looked out suspiciously, his hand on the door ready to shut it on us ; after a time, he let us in, on Mrs. H.'s persuasion. The room was full of shot-holes. The nurse was his mother—he was just eighteen, but hardly looked it. She was out, but might be back. He said, wearily, that he had been in the police-prison. Yes, at the Floridsdorf police-station, Tuesday to Friday. He had been beaten on the face. No, it didn't show now, but it had been badly swollen when he came back. But it didn't seem to bother him much ; what did bother him was that just before they drove him off there he had looked out of the window and seen his father lying dead on the pavement below. We asked about his mother, and were told she was "a 'Christian Socialist' nurse." I am not sure what that means, perhaps nothing much, politically—one can't enquire too closely into people's political views, these days. We talked vaguely of events ; people think there will be nothing to-morrow, when the Nazi ultimatum expires. The nurse did not come back. We said good-bye to Mrs. H.—we would come back to-morrow. Yes, it was all *furchtbar, furchtbar*. We walked back to the bus terminus. Gradually the things we could see from the jolting windows of our bus became normal

Dd

49

again : shops with gay dresses and flowers and gro-
ceries or sweets ; people walking briskly or strolling
pleasantly ; motor-cars ; elegance : the Gothic
cathedral.

We had lunch with a doctor's wife—very nice and
sympathetic—a Jewess, and so full of stories about
things which had happened to Jews—there are
certainly a few among the dead, though not very
many—and very fearful of the future. She had been
down to the Frauen-hilfe (Mme Dollfuss's fund)
that morning, but had found it shut. She had taken
some names to the Friends, but they said they could
do nothing. Had I heard that the Engels Hof was
being renamed (or should I say re-christened ?) the
Dollfuss Hof ? Lass's four-year-old boy asked questions hard all through lunch ; he seemed well up in
the political situation. He had quite enjoyed the
firing during the day, but at night had shown a
desire to keep his window shut. His pacifist mother
had to put up with him saying, " Yes, when I fight
people I shall be sure to have more guns than they
have." Both she and I were wildly tired ; luckily,
he felt like playing a game in which the grown-up
is shot dead (bang, bang) and covered restfully with
pieces of the *Manchester Guardian*. I wonder how much
he will remember of it ?

On the way back I was so tired that I lost my way.
The man I had met earlier, Evert, a research student
and, incidentally, special correspondent by his own
request, but most adequately, to that great paper,

the *Auchtermuchty Advertiser* (shall we say), came along and discussed things. He wanted some first-hand stuff, so I said I would take him along to Floridsdorf the next morning—a very fair exchange, for he talks excellent German and can interpret for me. Also, the wife of the Vienna correspondent of yet another great and famous newspaper, rang up and asked me to supper, which I accepted gladly. And then it was time to start again.

After my talk with Evert (who had seen Sam, as also Z, Y, X, and conceivably W—it's always like this in Wien !) I decided I must send home a wire about the T.U. fund—I had hoped for a telegram saying M. was coming, but there was nothing. It seemed extremely advisable to send a big name of some kind ; in my telegram I suggested Ponsonby. After sending that—but when it gets to London, people will just say, " Oh, Vienna seems to have gone to her head too ! "—I took the Floridsdorf bus again, walked through the darkening streets and over the railway bridge, and found my way to the Gemeinde Haus and the staircase of my friend Mrs. T. She opened at once, smiling.

It had been very exciting for me, going there by myself ; I sat in the bus, looking out and observing things—the beautiful sunset sky, and the horrid pictures of Dollfuss and the Vaterländische Front. My feet were sore ; I tried to think myself into a state of calm. But I was filled with a sense of pride which is hard to communicate, which some people

might laugh at, and some not understand. It was a
most unjustifiable pride—I had nothing to be proud
of, I knew that—simply the feeling that I was going
back to my own people. But I liked to be going
alone, and at sunset, and not knowing what I would
say, only that some workers whom I did not yet
know were going to call me comrade, and I was
going to call them comrade, and there would be
trust and acceptance. Foreknowing this, I said to
myself, rationally, that I was being silly, that I would
surely be disappointed of my sentimental dreams. I
was not disappointed.

My friend opened the door and brought me in,
quickly, to the flat. I am going to describe it. There
were three good-sized rooms ; the kitchen-dining-
room had a cooking recess for the stove and utensils
and sink, curtained off at will. This room had
linoleum, the other two had parquet floors ; the
passage was big enough to hold a large wardrobe
and oddments. The sitting-room had a square bow,
facing south, which could be opened all round in
summer, but had a glass door between it and the
main part of the room—it made a good little play-
room for the children. It was well furnished, though
rather over-elaborately ; it reminded me very much
of Bournville, though the pictures were pleasanter—
photographs of landscapes under deep snow mostly.
There was a big, carved oak dresser, with china and
glass, and a sofa, with a row of dolls and Teddy bears.
When I came in, the radio was in full blast ; it was

on a stand in the corner, and there was an embroidered cover on the stand. I think my friend
is so full of life and energy that she loves unnecessary
and elaborate things like embroidered covers. But
she has plenty to be energetic about now. I think this
is typical of the better flats in the Gemeinde Haus ;
I had noticed that many of them had flowers growing
in their bay windows, behind the glass—or had
before it was broken. There are all sorts of pleasant
amenities which the cheaper English houses lack—
plenty of electric-light points, well-fitting doors, and
so on. For this her husband pays twenty-five Austrian
Schillings a month.

I found out later that she had been married at
eighteen and was now twenty-four. But I did notice
not only how pretty her hair was without the hat,
but how long and thick her eyelashes were, and how
broad she was about the brows, with lovely, soft,
unplucked eyebrows. The three children were
playing about—a little girl of five, a boy of three,
and a baby ; we talked about them for a few minutes.
The little boy had been badly frightened, and had a
fever after the bombardment ; he looks pale still.
She asked me if I would like to see the flat. When I
was alone, I did what I meant to do ; I said, " Can
I trust you ? " She stiffened and nodded. I said, " I
am a party comrade from England—I come from
the party to help." She said, " Yes " ; and then,
" The others will come." I think she had been expecting me to say that, or something like it. When we

came back to the sitting-room, and the children were quiet, we began to talk ; she wanted to talk ; she wanted to tell someone everything. I don't know if she was right to trust me at once, but she did.

She told me first, that, out of this building alone, sixty-one are gone—*ausgeflogen*—more than forty have got to Brünn. Eight were killed on the frontier. I asked her about herself, straining my ears and mind to understand what she said, for she talked faster as she got more excited. She was not actually a party member (nor is her husband, who is in a bank), but she and he are both in strong sympathy. She has a cousin who is in a fountain-pen factory. At twelve on Monday came the Strike, and the cousin hurried back. At first there were no orders— they found that their *Führer*, their leaders, had been taken. They knew there were weapons somewhere, hidden away. The cousin and a few other *Genossen* had searched for them frantically. The weapons only came at eight ; the machine guns were mounted. They did not know yet, even, whether they had found all the weapons, probably there are still some hidden. They fought all Tuesday. Many of the civilians went, but she stayed. Several of the women took food and drink to the fighters. Her husband had been kept at the office—when he got out, he was told the house had been destroyed and she was dead ; she laughs about that now, because it's all right.

Tuesday, the Schutzbund retreated ; the machine

guns were dismounted and taken away. The Heim-wehr had brought up an armoured car, and by 4.30 the house was surrounded. After that there was no more firing, though it was on Wednesday morning early that the $4\frac{1}{2}$-inch howitzers began the bombard-ment and did most of the damage. The bombard-ment went on all Wednesday ; there were nearly a hundred shots—some were duds, and they were left in the house till Saturday. The army people would not touch them. By Wednesday most people had left the house—a few had already left on Tuesday, mostly going off to stay with friends. Those who were left were for the most part women and children whose men had disappeared. It was on Wednesday that most people were killed. No one knew why they went on firing back. Perhaps it was because no one had hoisted a white flag, or perhaps because Dollfuss came along that day, and they wanted to show him that they were doing something.

After that the men fled—most of them. Later I met one or two who hadn't, and had not yet been arrested; they were very gay about it. But some of the men, especially the older ones, the civilians who had not fought in the Schutzbund (it was mostly Schutz-bund men who had gone), were arrested and taken off to Floridsdorf police-station. She went there with food for them, while her mother looked after the sick child. There were forty-eight in a small room, about fifteen by six or eight (but one can't blame the police for that). She began to describe how they looked, the

55

heads and faces covered with blood ; she lifted her arms, like a man using a rifle butt as a club. It was mostly about the head and face that they were beaten ; one man had been beaten in the yard and then thrown down on the stones and his back broken. The police admitted to her that they had been killing some of the fire-brigade. She said to them, "That is not *menschlich*!" They said, "Yes, but there were not so many." The ordinary prisoners at the police-station got thin soup and bread three times a day. I have heard that some of them got nothing for two or three days, but at least it was all right for these ones.

She gave me isolated facts—or perhaps I only understood from time to time clearly. I remember the six dead who were left for four days ; the Heimwehr would not let the women come out to fetch them. There were twenty-five Heimwehr dead (but that may have been at the railway station). There were stories of other places—in the Brigitten Bezirk the Schutzbund prisoners were beaten to tell where they had hidden the weapons. The wife of a man killed at the Floridsdorf police-station had to sign a declaration saying that her husband had died the day before. From here there are about ten men missing whom no one knows anything at all about.

Then the cousin came in—a short, thick-set man, with eyes like hers but more grey than blue. I said again that I was a party comrade from England. He

said, " Are you from the Friends ? " I said, " No, I
am not even religious." He laughed, and said, " Nor
am I ! " I tried to explain that I am really a *Schrift-
steller*, but had come over before the official committee from the party, to try to help and to show
Solidarität. I had a little money, not official, but from
Arbeiter-Partei comrades. It was just to keep things
going. But he thought of me as the first of the English
Labour Party which was coming over to help at last.
To some extent I had to live up to that, to represent
for him, and those to whom he will speak of me, the
Labour movement of England and Scotland. After
all, why not ?

I asked if the Dollfuss fund had come here, but they
said not. There was nothing, and many people had
no money and no food, *absolut nichts*. There were
spies everywhere. Someone had taken a snapshot of
a Schutzbundler and then shown it to the police.
Others who might have betrayed did not. One of
the *Führer* had a son who was beaten to tell where
his father was ; he did not tell, but he was beaten
until he went mad.

The cousin produced some photographs, which he
gave me, and which I am hoping to get over to
England. There were two tramway-men ; one was
shot through the leg, and another was helping to get
him home. Then he was shot himself, and fell with
his friend. A doctor managed to get to them, and
took the first tramway-man into a cellar and put a
tourniquet of electric-lamp flex round his bleeding

leg. But the other man was dead. One photograph
showed him and yet another dead man lying against
the wall of the house. Other photographs showed
the smashed rooms. If I came back to-morrow, I
would see them. I said, " I will come back, but may
I bring another *Partei Genosse*, the journalist Evert ? "
I showed his card—they looked at the name of the
paper. I tried to explain the Scottish papers. They
said yes, he might come, but would I bring him
myself ?

Then another comrade came in, a boy who could
speak a little English. That was good, for my German
was getting tired. He was a nice, gentle boy, with a
merry face, dressed in a coat too big for him. His
father was still in prison—his sentence lasted till the
7th. Before that he had been unemployed, on and
off, since 1929. The boy had qualified for a skilled
job in 1932, but could not get it. And, bad enough
though it was then, now it would be impossible.
But at least he was alive, and, oh, so glad to see that
the English Arbeiter-Partei were sending at last !
Both he and the cousin are party functionaries—not
only were, but are still. The party is alive. Had I
seen any of their *Führer* ? " Yes," I said, but I gave
no names. They respected that in these days. They
spoke without bitterness of the leaders—rather with
love and loyalty. In detail the *Führung*—the leadership from moment to moment—may have been, and
probably was, wrong, but the *Führer*, the leaders,
there was nothing wrong with them. There was no

" betrayal of the workers." If only the Communist Party would realise that simple difference !

I asked if many in the party were going Nazi. " Yes," they said ; and the girl said, " They must ; they have to have revenge." But the men said, " No ; they must not." They were trying to keep the party together, but always leftward. Left, but in the party still. I tried to tell them about the Socialist League. But it all seems remote. And then they told me of a man who was found with weapons and dragged out of his flat to be shot. But his wife and children ran in front of him, and begged and prayed —and in the end they took him to prison instead. It was a comparatively cheerful story.

But then it was late, and I had to go and see some other families. We said, " Good-bye. Good-bye, comrades. Good luck. *Freundschaft. Freiheit !* " And I, seeing their faces, " If only I could say to you what is in my heart ! "

The girl and I went up a stair whose glass was shattered. " Look," she said, " a mouse—*ein Mauserl* ! " and her voice was all friendly to the mouse. She stooped to touch it as it scampered about the stair. She told me, when it came to the second family, that the man had been killed. I went in, feeling infinitely awkward, and began my speech about coming from England, trying to speak very gently. There was a woman sitting at one side of the table, a man at the other—her brother—neither of them speaking. On a stool, facing the wall, sat a

59

five-year-old girl, with fair, fine curls ; she stared at the wall, and her hands shook. I put the twenty Schillings into the woman's hand, and she stared and coloured, and began to cry. She caught at me : "*Küss' die Hand, gnädige Frau !*" And the awful thing was, she meant it. I was really coming between her and starvation. It's rather horrifying having one's hand kissed by a comrade in tears. She snatched up the child, and told her to kiss my hand—the child curtseyed—I picked her up and kissed her. She was a perfectly lovely child ; I didn't want to cry myself. I could still feel where my hand had been kissed.

The next place was in the other part of the house, by the clock tower. My friend and I walked through the courtyard ; in the moonlight the great, proud house looked more beautiful than I can say. Two policemen came out of an arch ; my friend and I caught one another round the neck, and each said to the other, " Do not be frightened ! " The police went by ; we went through an arch. The towers and square cliffs of the Gemeinde Haus were still beautiful, but, under the moon, the shell-holes looked horribly black and ragged. In this house there was another woman whose husband had been killed. I had several more names, but could not wait to see them as it was already so late.

We said good-bye till to-morrow, and I walked away towards the street ; a man spoke suddenly at my elbow ; I saw, in the moonlight, that he was the brother of the woman with the flaxen-haired child. He said, " I have left my sister crying, partly because of what has happened, but mostly because she knows now that we are not alone—we have not been forgotten." And he said, " It seemed as though no one knew." We walked on together—he a heavy, garlic-smelling man. I said, " It is so little." He : " That does not matter ; better little and a good heart." I said, " Soon my party will send more ; it is difficult." He : " Yes, there is always bureaucracy in parties." And then he looked up at the little shops and houses we were passing—sham French or sham baroque— and he said, " The people from these houses came and smashed our beautiful houses that we workers had built ; they want everyone to have no better houses than this ; they have broken our beautiful houses ! " And so we came to the bus stop, in the square of little single bourgeois houses and shops, and he put his face very close to mine—we had been walking close together, especially when we passed the police—and he whispered, " *Freundschaft* ! " And he was gone.

And I went back to Vienna, desperately foot-sore, but nearly crying with joy, and the pride of earlier on fulfilled beyond my former knowledge. It was one of the moments when one knows for certain that everything is worth while ; that events are not unconnected ; that there is a music and reason and kindness in history ; that this is the thing one has waited for—this, at last, is living. I have had much love in my life, and my new-born children laid in my arms, and I have had fame and praise and a lot of fun, but I don't think I have ever been happier than I was then.

But it was late, and, though I scuttled into clean clothes, I was quite a lot late for dinner with G., the correspondent of that famous paper. However, he was later still, and this is a nice friendly place where it doesn't matter being late. His wife is a platinum blonde—very like some film star, only I have forgotten which—and intelligent, though she seems to try and hide this. There was a much younger girl, pretty, very English, and the man she was going to marry—all romantically in Vienna of the " Blue Danube "—who was in the army, or just out of it. They seemed improbable after Floridsdorf. I felt myself remote. I tried to be extra polite ; the man didn't like me, but I think the girl did. I think she felt that after all there is something about this Socialism—but she didn't quite know what. Then G. himself came in, with a charming dog which put its feet on the table—we'd just been having an awfully good pudding. At first I thought he was remote too, and unreal and like his newspaper and all other newspapers, which are so successful at interposing themselves between oneself and reality. He gave me *Himbeer* brandy, saying it was the favourite drink of Starhemberg. But, in the other room, and especially after the others had gone— the girl looking ravishing in a Viennese hat, a honeymoon hat almost—he became completely real. He had written various things which show that he has an admirable grasp of realities, and has in general been a good chap. And he gave me some good advice, which I shall take. But I liked him not for being useful, or even for having such nice dogs, but for having such goodwill. How can it possibly go on being such an idiotic world when there are so many people of goodwill in it ?

Thinking that, I lost my way walking back—as usual. I was tired as anything, and only wrote a couple of letters, saying for once what I really felt, and let Evert know that it was O.K. about Floridsdorf.

FEBRUARY 28TH

I got up early, still aching about the feet. I had a blister, so perhaps it's as well that there seems to be no time to have a bath ! Also they cost three Austrian Schillings. I got some money that Sam wanted, partly for legal defence for party people, and some for myself for Floridsdorf. Then I went off with Evert. It is great fun being even a sham journalist, being at least taken for granted in this demi-monde of correspondents. Or have I got it all wrong, and do they really think, Damn it all, another interfering female ? No, I think it's O.K. We discussed all kinds of things—politics and our native city, and its gossip—and came, this time by tram, to the terminus. At the house, our friend was waiting for us again. Evert fell for her almost as rapidly as I did. Though whether his mature judgment is to be trusted over anyone with eyes like hers, I'm not sure. Actually, it's fun going about with anyone as young as he is ; he makes one feel that after all one isn't such a sentimental adolescent, since he, with all the glorious grown-upness of those who have ceased to be undergraduates for at least a year, is just as silly as one is oneself.

Another young man came along too, with some more small photographs of the smashed buildings. He said that the windows are being officially mended !—otherwise there's been no help. The Frauen-Hilfe hasn't appeared here. Or rather, after the first day or two someone came round and made sympathetic noises, but nothing has come of it. The Dollfuss-Innitzer fund is only for the wounded. (I am not saying that this is true, but it's the impression the people themselves have got.) Everyone in municipal services have lost their pensions. As to the Vaterländische Front—he could tell us, for instance, of a private concern, safe-makers, who had said that anyone not joining must " take the consequences." In the gas and the electricity works those who worked the Strike were all turned out, and gradually other party members, who played a more passive part, are being turned out too. A hundred and fifty have been dismissed from the electricity, twenty-five have been dismissed from the gas works, for not joining the Vaterländische Front—and they will probably have their unemployment pay stopped too. It is all pretty thorough.

Again, people are constantly being arrested through the treachery of their neighbours, who betray them to the police, perhaps for pay, but mainly so that they themselves will not be arrested. The police don't know themselves who they have arrested, and who they haven't. We went on talking, Evert making notes ; they liked him—liked thinking that another English Partei Genosse had come to them. They wanted to know what the English party thinks of Austria. But how am I to explain the thought processes of Transport House ?

We walked some way together, through streets and across the railway. This was where some of the earliest fighting was ; there isn't a house unmarked. In this building, the howitzer shells had dropped in the courtyard and spattered the inner walls with metal. There were burnt marks in the grass where three had exploded, and heaps of broken glass everywhere—hardly a whole pane. On the first staircase we went up, all the doors had been forced, though obviously half the flats were facing so that no one could have been shooting out of them. Up in the attic there was a fearful mess where a direct hit had

burst ; it was only a store-place, there were toy rails
there, a push-cart, a bird-cage, but they had apparently thought it was a machine-gun emplacement.
Evert was much more surprised and shocked than
I was by the shell-holes ; he was as unused to that
kind of thing as the gentle Viennese—the younger
ones. But it seemed all very familiar to me ; I kept on
thinking of the early war photographs—Belgian
atrocities and all that. It was definitely *war*, of
course. The door of the attic above the next floor
had been bombed in case anyone had been there ;
that had made a nasty mess too. Very few of the
dwellers in these houses are insured—under five per
cent. No wonder the windows aren't being mended
very quick.

On another staircase we went into a flat where the
kitchen was all right and one bedroom not so bad,
but in the children's bedroom there had been a direct
hit, and everything was incredibly smashed up. I
picked up a couple of scribbled drawings by one of
the children ; they and their mother had gone into
the passage beyond five minutes before the hit.
The woman has heard nothing from any fund so far,
but, as her husband is not in prison, things aren't
too bad there. They go on living in the flat.

At the top of another stair were two completely
smashed flats. The gas-stove was crinkled like paper,
the partition walls were all down. Most of the furniture was unrecognisable. But I picked up a copy of a
paper, the *Heimatschützer*, the Heimwehr paper. The

man had been an old Social Democrat—he was a railwayman—then gone Nazi, then Heimwehr. And then judgment had come upon him. I took some paper flowers and a bit of a plaster ornament. Above, again, was a studio and offices—some of the top flats had been made into the most lovely studios. Here a direct hit had got one end, and another had gone right through at the far end. Everything was smashed and twisted, and covered with plaster dust ; there were Christmas-tree branches, with pieces of silver spangle on them—old letters. The man's paintings had all been in a canvas bag, and a shell had gone through it. Again it was a judgment, for the man, who had once been a Socialist, had gone Nazi—the Nazi paper was lying on the floor.

We came down the stair and out into the court ; there were a lot of children playing there, including the little girl whose drawings out of the smashed room I had in my pocket. She was pretty, fair, and blue-eyed, a seven-year-old, and a great friend of our guides. She wore a plush coat and a striped cap, and she looked rather white, but seemed very jolly ; I wonder how much it has really affected them ? We passed the wash-house, where a couple of bombs had been chucked, on general principles, and then went on to the part of the house from which actual firing had taken place. We went up a stair, and into the worst smash yet : one flat which had been empty, but, beside it, another where four people had been— father, mother, and two children. At 7 a.m. on

Wednesday, the day after all firing had ceased from the house, the guns opened fire from the far bridge—the one we had crossed. The four were all in bed. The mother was wounded in the stomach and breast, and died of wounds ; the father is still very ill ; one of the children has lost a foot. They were Social Democrats, but, as the father was a small functionary of some sort, he had never been active. Now the four rooms of the flat were indescribably littered with remains—bricks and pieces of wood and a woman's bag and an umbrella and a cross-word and a calendar, and a lot of children's books and half a doll and a hoop and Christmas-tree candles, and dried-up remains of the cacti which the Viennese so much like putting into their windows.

The other flat was the same, and, looking out from its window, we saw another smashed flat, and noticed that it was still occupied. The inhabitants have nowhere else to go. We went on, right up, past store-rooms, where a shell had burst, up a ladder, and out on to the roof, which has a superb view over the Danube and the city and far out to the hills where there are still patches of snow. Incidentally it commands the approach to the railway bridge from this end and the road between it and the Floridsdorf police-station. The roof was still littered with spent cartridges ; I looked at a lot of them, and found they were dated any year between 1913 and 1918, but never, as far as I saw, beyond. No sort of rush for armaments during the last year or two !

There was also a pail of water, which had been used for cooling, and the ropes which had kept it fast.

This had been a machine-gun post during the Tuesday, but by Tuesday evening it had been moved back in the gradual abandonment of this front. There were only two machine-gun posts—the police insisted that there were six. One couldn't help feeling un-pacifist about it.

Our friends explained that for twenty-four hours no one had been left in the houses—everyone was turned out for the search. During that time, looting happened, and, when people were allowed back, all sorts turned up and said they were the owners, when they weren't, and stole things. It would certainly be wrong to impute all the looting to the Heimwehr and the police. They showed us the place where the railway-men had been shot and the dead man had lain for days. The ground was still unpleasantly discoloured. It was now nearly two, so I gave my friend one hundred and thirty Schillings for the people whose names were on her list ; she said she would rather not give me a receipt, and I said, " Of course not." I think she can be trusted completely. Then we said, " Auf Wiedersehen." I said I'd try and come round on Friday.

After that, Evert and I lunched, hungrily, and then went off to find ——, to whom I had a letter. After much searching, we found a dim little street and a back staircase, a room rather like a bad street in Selly Oak or North Kensington, an old man and woman, but no ——, he having had warning that morning. However, X offered to take us to see W., who had taken on his job since the morning, and we started off. Evert has an engaging British habit of talking rather loud in trams, while poor X was already conditioned to whispering. They weren't saying anything particularly secret, but I think X was a bit worried ! The Dollfuss posters were stamped over in red with, " I Am a Murderer "— by Nazis. X seemed to approve. He explains that the Government are trying to confiscate the Social Democrat funds " for repairing damages " ; but it has now been discovered that this really belongs to Socialists in Belgium, that to the Second International, and so on. It remains to be seen whether Dollfuss is bold enough to confiscate it all the same (seeing they are only Socialists, although foreigners).

We found W., a small man with a nervously bold manner, and asked him to come and see us to-morrow. Then back to the hotel, just in time for me to go to the newspaper office to meet G., whom I like increasingly. We went on from there to the office of still another important English newspaper, and found its correspondent faintly nervous, as a result of this and that, and full of good advice. But he spoke as a journalist, whereas my friend G. speaks as a chap—and that makes all the difference. We discussed news ; they were both, of course, anxious for everything to be quite authentic, and one understands that ; the difficulty is that almost anything must necessarily be second-hand—the police don't come out and beat their prisoners in front of one.

Dinner with Sam—in a charming *Keller* full of jolly-looking students, mostly girls. Afterwards I had settled to write when Evert came in with news that —— and —— were going to be beaten up or run out of the country—would I go to the Legation the next morning early, and see what could be done ? It was now nearly two in the morning, and I had looked forward to a quiet morning during which I could (*a*) sleep, and (*b*) write some articles and finish my diary, and I felt I didn't much care *who* was beaten up. However, I promised to get up and go, and, inwardly cursing —— and ——, went to sleep. This, by the way, is the day when the original Nazi ultimatum was supposed to be going to come—the truce is ended. But nothing has happened. I suppose the Nazis feel they needn't really bother ; the place will drop into their mouths, anyhow.

MARCH 1ST

A rather unsatisfactory day ! I went off to the Legation, taking a taxi, it was so late, and presented an introduction. It was a large and stately place, and curiously part of another world. I was " received with courtesy "—there's no other phrase—and got no change at all. I was told that I had only brought a canard (as I probably had), and when I then went on to ask about the prisoners and whether nothing was going to be done about, for instance, releasing Professor Adler, I was met with a political and economic lecture. They had a large and impressive coloured map, and, of course, it was all very sound, but, oh dear, we were talking different languages ! And somehow I seem to have forgotten the kind of public-school and university language which Legations talk ; it was all from the head, and I had been living with the heart. I expect the *Realpolitik* was all perfectly sound—once one admits certain conditions of mind—but it never quite came real to me. And I can't feel that there is even that much to be said for Dollfuss. No doubt he has a very difficult time, but—— And, while I was there, I was interested to observe that the correspondent of *The Times* rang up. Not, of course, that there was any reason why he shouldn't. And after a time I went away.

I tried hard to get some stuff written in time to go

away to England, but it was no use. Lass turned up and then ——, ——, and ——, not to speak of the others. Quite a committee ; we discussed relief work, but I am afraid I can't put down what was decided, partly because it seems most inadvisable, even to me, and partly because everyone talked German very hard and fast, and I simply got lost. All the sentences seemed to go on for ever, and then end with an irregular verb which I never, somehow, knew.

Then lunch with Sam, Evert, and Lass, during which the males became very particular about what they ate, and the females rather scornful. Then to Sam's where I met —— (not the same, but another), and promised her a rather peculiar kind of help. Then back, to write letters and diary ; and to try vainly to telephone to Dick—but I suppose he wasn't there. One feels curiously isolated here in this lunatic asylum ; nobody in England, except detective-story writers, can imagine it—and I wanted to get in touch with nice, cool, sane England. There is a treble atmosphere of conspiracy : the atmosphere of Floridsdorf, where everyone is on edge still from the smashing up and in constant fear of betrayal and re-arrest ; the atmosphere of the men and women who are on the run, but are still full of hope and excitement and constant planning, who meet secretly in dark rooms and whisper, and are constantly verifying one another—Is he all right still ? —Is the new one for certain a comrade ?—and finally the atmosphere of the other kind of conspirators who meet in the largest and most expensive cafés, surrounded by other conspirators of all nations, not to speak of police spies. Personally, I find one tends to drift into the second category ; when our friends turned up and held their little committee, I shut the window as carefully as any conspirator !

We had another talk with G., who was admirably cheery. Then I went up to supper with . . . . and his nice Scottish wife. The atmosphere there was distinctly more like Bloomsbury, if it were possible to imagine a Bloomsbury in which it was really brave or dangerous to be a Communist. The criticism was much the same, and so was the lack of immediate constructiveness, but things were just that much more real. I'm not sure what my own attitude toward the C.P. should be, whether there is a case for united front, or whether it isn't still more important to have Social Democrat Party solidarity. In this present fog of suspicion, one has probably to keep as clear as possible—from as many people as possible ! It was a superb night, a full moon, and not cold.

I came back and started writing. Evert came round, and we decided that I might as well write a *Herald* article, which I did, ending with an appeal for funds. I sent it, with three photographs and a letter, unsigned, to Sylvia, and, by the same post, a letter to Dick, comparatively innocuous. (I've decided to stay on here, rather than take a room, as

I am really less conspicuous in a hotel than anywhere else.) Evert took it round to the air-mail ; it went registered, which means that it must be taken open, so that the girl at the post can see that no money is being sent out. Then one seals it, and it is fairly safe. Though I don't think anything is quite safe.

I had got a letter from Denny, really speaking out about his Nazi school, having been very careful not to say anything of the sort before. It decided me to stay on and go back with him—unless I get turned out first.

Evert came back from the post, and I made tea ; it felt quite like Russia. It was past midnight, and when he said he was not going to be called I felt bitterly jealous of him ! However, some day I hope even to have time for a bath. We talked a bit about Greece and nice sunny things.

MARCH 2ND

To-day, first to Sam's, and then, by 8.30, to pick up Lass at her small boy's school. A possibility had arisen that I might be going to do some V.A.D. work, as it were, so I asked her to help me to buy gauze and bandages in the least suspicious manner. What a boy-scout, Red-Indian business it all is !

We went along to the Schlinger Hof. We'd meant to go round with the *Fürsorgerin*, but decided finally that we had better not (this was confirmed later by Mrs. H.) as she might be really a " Christian Socialist." Lass had an enormous list of people, again, but some were out when we called. The first were in some tenement buildings belonging to the railway, not nearly so good as the Gemeinde Hauser, though still not so bad as some of the private enterprise blocks. Here the rents vary from nine to fifteen Austrian Schillings a month for two- or three-roomed flats.

It was amazing how quickly they picked things up, once they had got over their first suspicions. Lass said, almost in inverted commas, that we were " strangers, of no party," but in a few minutes they were treating us as definitely of their party. I think the solidarity got across all right. The first house was a widow, with one son " gone " ; then there was a woman whose man was back, after two spells of prison—he looked as though he'd been through something. But here they had been helped already, I suspect by the party, from the way they said it, and they were definitely not going to try and get any more. They were very friendly, though.

In another room, the husband—one of the men driven out from the Schlinger Hof into the street— was home, but still with a bullet in his back. He was a great strong man, a butcher's assistant, but goodness knows what he will do now. There is a baby three weeks old. They'd had no help, and seemed to expect none. The difficulty at the moment is that the rents are falling due—they mostly did not pay their half-monthly rent due a fortnight ago, but they will probably have to pay now. I admire these houses more and more ; there is no lowering of standards about them. In so many English model dwellings all the paint is mud-coloured or greenish, as suitable for the poor, and there are skimpy iron banisters, while here there is lots of white paint, and brass, and nice wooden handrails.

We went on to see my friend, who had several more cases ; we discussed which could be given to the Friends, safely, as we cannot go on indefinitely ourselves. But we can't pass on any names which might be bad if they fell into the hands of the police. Even the Friends are rumoured not safe—they wouldn't give things away themselves, but a search is not an impossibility. We left eighty Schillings for her to distribute.

Back in Vienna, we were both frightfully hungry and went into a café, had coffee with cream, and read the *Vie Parisienne*. It seems curious how, when so many of the readers of that excellent little café-journal are women, there should be no alluring pictures of men in it. One very rarely sees a picture of a man made to look specifically alluring. Though no doubt they exist. Conceivably one might be shocked ; I wonder ? On our way, this morning, we passed a shop-window in which the wax ladies were undecided as to what they were going to wear that

77

day; they had nothing on but stockings. Do the English wax ladies always re-dress during the darkest hours of the night? Or are they modestly taken into a back room? Or have they permanent petticoats?

We picked up Jake from his school, and bought our bandages and things, which were all very expensive. This is an expensive town, largely, I suppose, because almost everything has to be imported. Fruit is ridiculously dear. I want to get an ordinary little black hat, but I don't know where to get it—they don't seem to go in much for large stores. And there is a distressing absence of Woolworths. Jake pulled us up to look in at a toy-shop; apparently all the Vienna shops are sold out of toy cannons in the last week or two!

Saw my old west-coast friend, Ian—very much upset over a paragraph in the *Herald*, saying that all the relief money is to go through the Friends. If this is so, there will be nothing left for the people who can't or won't give their names except to the party, and nothing for legal aid for prisoners, not to speak of other things. The others were all badly bothered about it too. But perhaps it isn't true; it may be a blind for the authorities here. But in this game of double-crossing one never knows which is black and which is white.

I came back to the hotel, to find several telephone messages, and an urgent note from an unknown man. After lunch the unknown turned up, a nice young

Cambridge Communist, all " het up " about some of the Reichstag prisoners, and wanting to know if I or anyone I knew could fly at once to Berlin and see about it. I suggested various people in London whom he could ring up, though goodness knows that's dangerous enough. I gather that all telephone calls to *Ausland* are listened to, though no doubt they don't always quite understand. In the middle the brother of one of these men turned up, dark and white-faced and little, hunted-looking, like some nice pathetic animal, a dark-eyed hare perhaps ; probably his brother is being tortured by the Nazis. A horrid world. I could do nothing.

I had been round again to try and see Ian and ask him if the unknown man was all right—one gets into that habit, and one can't very well use the telephone where proper names are involved. He was out, but the girl from next door, who opened the door, turned out to be a sister of my neighbour Gert, and very sympathetic.

MARCH 2ND: EVENING

Out again, saw Ian, talked about Scotland, and discussed the young unknown, what we could do for him and he for us. The local C.P. are of course full of spies, fuller than any other party ; one has to be ridiculously careful. Then on to get my money from Cook's, but, like a fool, I didn't verify the address from my old Baedeker, so, by the time I had discovered that it was no longer in the Stephans Platz, it was too late to go to the right place. I came back, incredibly tired, rang up the young man, and asked him to come round ; he couldn't, so reluctantly I decided I must go round to him—after all, the information I had might conceivably be a slight means of saving someone's life. But I was too tired for anything but taxis—and he lived at an address no taxi seemed to know. I found him at last, with a Viennese wife—a dark, untidy comrade—neither of them looking very domesticated. He strikes me as too gentle to be a good politician. Probably the best politicians of all are really tough women.

I came back, aching with tiredness, black under the eyes. I have forgotten again to ask them to give me honey for breakfast (though I have arranged for a Schilling off my room price) ; I expect I shall go on forgetting now I've started. I ought to write my *New Statesman* article ; I started, but it turned out all wrong. I'm too tired, *müde, ich bin so müde*. It's so worrying that the traffic here all keeps to the left ; when one goes to a foreign town one expects it to be going the wrong way. I bought half a kilo of oranges, one doesn't get fruit much, and it's not awfully good when one does. Evert is coming round to have tea, but not so late as usual, for I've got to sleep. He and I can shout to one another easily across the courtyard, if only there was a little more time for romance, we might throw one another roses—at any rate our typewriters click in time !

.   .   .   .

I have had a bath, and left the most shaming black mark round the top. I ought to have got some meth. to rub on my feet. Oh, dear, I do hope no one more will ring up.

MARCH 3RD

Slept till 9.45. Black under the eyes gone, and blisters on feet better. Breakfast in bed—and I did ask for honey ! Janet tells me there may be need of my V.A.D. services to-morrow, not to-day. She herself is seeing a lot, and is probably already suspect. I had begun the day lazily by reading in bed, Gedye's *Heirs to the Habsburgs*, which is extremely enlightening on past history. People are always saying, " You remember what happened in 1927, don't you ? " And I never do. After all, Austria seemed a long way off then ; there was probably a drought in England, or something. But after Janet came, I felt I must be energetic again. I went to Cook's, and collected the money, from R. and H. ; I wonder if my law-abiding H. will like the way his money is likely to go ! But people in England just can't understand one's feeling here, the way illegality begins to appear obvious and ordinary. Cook's is in the most prosperous part of Vienna, the Kärtner Ring, next the biggest hotels and luxury shops ; the morning was filled with a bright and opulent sun. People were strolling. I noticed, at the tram stops, the big photographs of the Gemeinde Hauser, mostly in summer, with their bathing-pools and children playing on the grass. These are being pulled down now, and more ordinary Viennese attractions put up instead at the tram stops.

There were soldiers about again. Sometimes they pull machine guns with them, in little push-carts ; you wouldn't believe these things were really meant to kill. Some of the young men in uniform aren't Heimwehr but some other kind of Catholic young loyalist.

Sam came in with some more stuff, a direct translation of a letter from a man who had been beaten up in prison and seen it happen to others. I said I'd get it off, and an article for *Time and Tide*. I must also send part of my diary and various letters. It's this working against time which is difficult.

I went over to the —— Café, as arranged, to meet Y (whose real name, as a matter of fact, I don't know !). I was five minutes late, owing to the bursting of one of those essential elastics which keep the modern woman together (or don't), but U, V, and Y himself were ten or twenty minutes late. I am getting used to that ; it's like Russia—one's Western-time concepts don't hold. I go about always with a Baedeker, it seems to me to constitute a perfectly good disguise, and the map is useful—and it is funny to read about the things one ought to see, which don't seem to include the Gemeinde Hauser.

After some telephoning, we started, going up into the Ottakring district, which was a sixty to seventy per cent Socialist district. It was not unlike an out-lying Paris *banlieue*—high houses, small shops, Victorian ornament, tram-lines. We got out of our tram, and walked. We passed a worker's library. This has now been closed, with all other party works, and will not be reopened until it has been cleansed, in the high German fashion, of all Socialist or other corrupting works. We then came to the side-street in which stands the Arbeiterheim of Ottakring, a building put up by the party before the War, for meetings, conferences and so on, with its own theatre and a great hall. The two streets on to which it looked, back and front, were closed. The Heimwehr sentry wouldn't let us pass. I then said I was sure I could go on my own, so I went round another way—there were crowds everywhere, standing as near as they could get, and staring—one couldn't tell what they thought : it was a sight.

I produced my English passport, and said I was a journalist—I had written *Week-End Review* on a visiting-card, in case I wanted that too ! I also said how sad it would be if I had to tell my journal that they wouldn't let me through. I also put on my best innocent smile. Anyway, they let me through. I strolled along the street, and looked at the Arbeiter-heim, which is completely and irretrievably smashed. It must have had twenty or thirty direct hits from small shells at a near range. It looked as if one had gone through each window. I suppose most of the interior is burnt out, but one couldn't see. It was built at a bad period, and the theatre building had nymphs and graces standing about, with scrolls and things all over its front. One kallipygous lady had a bit of her behind chipped off. The whole place is ruined, but I believe the defenders all got away.

Half-way down the street I found a policeman in a blue uniform and a rifle. I remarked that it was *schwer*. He replied sympathetically. Seeing he was about forty, I remarked that it was just like the war. He answered that it was very sad, and there had been no need.

I rejoined our anonymous comrades, and we walked on to look at the various Gemeinde Hauser in the district. Everywhere were new advertisements of the Heimwehr—or rather of all the various sections of respectable opinion, anti-Socialist and anti-Nazi, and not quite knowing how best to be both. There is one which appeared for the first time, to my know-ledge, the day before yesterday, which shows pictures of machine guns and bombs in Gemeinde Hauser.

It is generally said that they were built as fortifications—much like the " concrete gun emplacements " which were found in August 1914 wherever anyone had a German governess. It is all the sillier about the houses, because when they were first built the respectable newspapers attacked them, saying they were so shoddy that they would fall down at the first rain-storm !

We passed the Schuhmeier Hof and others, mostly very well built, in a pleasing modern form, and of good materials—obviously planned to give the maximum amount of light and air to the inhabitants. Y tells me that in the old days the unemployed could get off paying rent, for a time anyhow. Now all this will be changed. Even if the houses aren't sold to private people, they will certainly be run at a profit. In this district there were Gemeinde Hauser everywhere. Altogether I believe they have built about 60,000 flats in Vienna, during the last ten years, housing, I suppose, four times that number of people. Families with young children got the preference, but there are—or were—still waiting-lists.

We went on to the Sandleiten, a great big place, like a model town, housing perhaps 5,000 families—a Greek city-state. They were mostly Social Democrats, just because the kind of people who lived in those kind of buildings mostly were Social Democrats—normally only those with a factory worker's income, or less, got on to the waiting lists—but it

wasn't necessary to be a party member to get a flat.
Sandleiten is built on a hill. The lower part is a great
double cliff of high flats, with bath-houses, kindergarten, and so on enclosed. But it is all built with a
pleasant irregularity, which makes it human, and
which also no doubt stops the feeling of complete
uniformity among the flats. Then comes a street
with a café, theatre, and so on, and a lot of small
shops, including a Co-op., as usual, all well designed.
Then a big, irregular-shaped piazza, with flats
standing all round it, and inlaid in the middle with a
stone pattern showing the points of the compass.
Then, higher up, were steps and a fountain, and
smaller flats, built in gardens round the Jugend-
hort—a building for the older children above school
age, where they can read, play games, make things,
and so on. These houses are connected by well-made
paths, with occasional steps, and here and there is a
wooden seat overlooking a lawn or a playing-place.
The winter grass is still colourless, and still there are
heaps of dirty snow here and there, melting by day
and hardening again by night, but in spring it should
be green and lovely, and the flowering bushes—
forsythia and prunus and spiræa—will colour every
bank and corner. Already the young birch-trees
have a purple bloom on them. These smaller houses,
each with four to six flats, mostly with balconies,
must be very pleasant to live in. They are made of
pleasantly treated concrete, either used as rough
artificial stone, or with a texture like fine harling ;

there is some simple decoration in concrete, just sufficient to formalise the houses against their environment of birch-trees and winding paths. The whole thing reminded me a little of Port Meirion. It was a definitely William-Ellisish effect.

We passed down, by steps and paths—a splendid play-ground for children—by a school, architected on what we are used to think of as very modern lines, with flat roofs and wide stretches of window, by a kindergarten, and by more of the higher blocks of flats. There was nothing elaborate or affected about the architecture, only the most obvious materials were used, concrete and tiles, everything was done in the interests of the inhabitants ; it is modernism, thoroughly domesticated for living-places. The whole place was built between 1924 and 1927. The only thing one has against it, on the grounds of comfort, is that the flats have no baths, and there is no central heating, although, as far as the latter is concerned, an unheated room, with double windows, next a kitchen with a stove in it, is fully as warm as an English room, with ordinary sash windows, heated by a coal fire. If the flat has an extra living-room beside the kitchen-dining-room, it almost certainly has a stove in the corner for heating. As to the bathroom, none of these people in all probability had such a thing in any of their previous homes, nor have most small middle-class flats in Vienna got anything so luxurious. It is even possible that in England we set too high a value by our

87

baths ; man cannot, after all, live by sanitation alone. Personally, I should dislike the idea of bringing up small children in a bath-less house ; but after the age at which one can adequately wash oneself—seven or so—which is also the age at which one ceases to be always so very dirty, it is not so difficult, and, although I should no doubt grumble very much, I should live quite happily so long as I had, say, a grand weekly bath in a bath-house, which is probably what people in the Gemeinde Hauser have. It is all largely a matter of clean linen ; I have an idea that we in England, with all our baths, tend to change our under-clothes less often than people do in comparatively bath-less countries. Still, I can't see any Labour member suggesting a building scheme which didn't allow for a bath to every family.

We walked from Sandleiten past a dozen other Gemeinde Hauser, built any time from 1923 to 1933. Architects of all schools have been employed, so that sometimes one sees stark modernism, with the pleasing and exciting vertical line of staircase windows, and sometimes something more in the old German style. Occasionally there is a definitely rather ugly house with unsuccessful decoration, but this is rare. Most of them would make one glad and proud to live in them. And I suppose this is what really annoys the middle classes, not so much that these buildings were built out of a house-tax and are not, therefore, economically sound by bourgeois standards of economics, but that people who are poor, and should therefore live in humility, have been given something to be proud of. That would account for their having wanted to hang Burgomaster Seitz, the Socialist mayor, when he was first taken. But even the Government jibbed at that.

The entrances to the houses have usually been made the occasion for a good piece of architectural decoration ; sometimes there is an adequate piece of statuary, usually a fine view through an archway. There are still notices posted up outside—in one place we saw the notice of a weekly party section meeting, with " Read the *Arbeiter Zeitung,*" but I suppose someone will discover that soon and pull it down. And in two or three places, low down on the wall, someone had chalked the Three Arrows, the sign of the Schutzbund here, and of the Socialist International throughout the world. It is amazing how a thing like that has the power suddenly to get at whatever part of one is the romantic centre. There is some old magic about it—as old as the swastika—" Three, three for the Arrows."

As we walked, we discussed what was the moral of all this for us—for England. My friends are Left-wingers, youngish men (the woman comrade had left us earlier on, looking a little odd, because she would keep putting on about twice too much face powder), and they were sadly, though not bitterly, critical. There is no question but that Deutsch and

Bauer are still believed in and trusted by their party. But there is also no question but that they temporised too long, on humanitarian grounds, so that their own people had lost heart before the struggle began, through seeing themselves constantly losing ground. It is, I think, conceivable that if the General Strike had been held—competently started and competently and firmly carried out, if necessary with violence—three months ago, the Social Democrats might have won and stopped the Heimwehr from getting power. But I think it most unlikely that this could have been done quite peaceably—though no doubt there would have been fewer deaths than there have been in the last three weeks—and, supposing it had been the Socialists who had " started a civil war," think of the pious hands raised in horror, the stern language by the Powers, the probability of intervention ! Austria is isolated. These things can be carried off in a country like Russia, which is almost self-supporting, and at any rate not surrounded by powerful and comparatively rich neighbours. It was not possible here. Bauer's policy was probably inevitable. And for us in England, in face of a growing Fascism, not yet, but perhaps in a few years—— ?

I asked how it was that the original Socialist Government in Austria had gone no further, immediately after the war, when it really did have the power. The answer, of course, was that the soldiers of the Entente were there. If the Socialists had done what

they wanted, had made a really Socialist State out of
Austria, the Entente would have cried Red Peril and
smashed them. Also, of course, they were starving.
They were near starving in Leningrad, too, in 1917 ;
but there the only help lay with themselves. Here,
the Entente would feed them—at a price : the price
of moderation and humility. Yet it might have been
better in the end if they had forced their Socialist
State on to Europe through blood and fire. Or was
that quite impossible ? Perhaps it was. Probably it
was. The Entente could have stopped it. The
Entente was Italy, not then Fascist, but partly, at
least, Socialist and syndicalist : France, republican
and democratic : and us, England, Liberal and
Labour, and believing in free speech and the rights
of man. Not to speak of America, still officially full
of noble professorial ideals of the self-determination
of small nations. One feels guilty here in Vienna ;
the Peace Guilt, worse than any War Guilt, is on
us.

So we walked through Ottakring and the next
district, looking at everything, wondering about the
future. What, for instance, would the new Catholic
administration do about the splendid municipal
bathing-pools ? Will there be no more mixed bathing
next summer ? We walked through the Linden Hof,
one of the finest of the Gemeinde Hauser. How soon
would the rents go up ? Would they be sold to private
contractors and companies, to have profits made out
of them ? The whole idea of that makes one squirm

with shame—as though these beautiful houses were beautiful women.

I agreed to go and see Y on Tuesday. There was some difficulty about this, as he could not bear the idea of my writing his address, even after seeing how illegible my handwriting is. However, at last he consented to my underlining the name of his street in my Baedeker map and writing the number at the other end. But not his name.

Back at the hotel I had an hour and a half to write. I finished my article for *Time and Tide*, and a letter to Lady Rhondda, to send with it. I am sending duplicates of this and the *New Statesman* article, but the copy that I send from here has no signature to the letter, nor address. I also started writing home about various things. Then I went off to the station, to meet M. and C. I managed to miss them, mainly through my own incompetence, but that made it no less annoying. They said they'd come down later. The hotel hold me that the Herr Doktor (that's to say Evert) was down in the *Keller*. They are getting quite sentimental about him and me ! I went down —it was now nearly nine—and the first person I saw was Z (whom I shall now, I think, call Anne). I grinned at her enquiringly, not sure if she wanted to be recognised or not ; however, it was all right, and she came and joined Evert and me ; later her boy-friend came too. They had just had bad news from the frontier, but were being exceedingly brave about it. It was rather a funny meal, all the same, because

Evert talked in his usual Oxford voice, which has a high carrying power, and whenever the waiters came, as they constantly did, the others tried to shut him up. However, I think the voice is really quite sound, because it sounds superbly unconspiratorial, and goodness knows it's refreshing in this hush-hush atmosphere !

I dashed off to get on with my typing, and then M. and C. turned up, with their hostess, looking as lovely as ever, and Viennese in the traditional sense that I have almost forgotten. Then Sam turned up, and we all went up to my room, and had a committee.

Somehow, we had all hoped that M. would have come with the English money. I suppose we ought to have known that Transport House never does anything in a hurry, but over here three weeks seems rather a long time. She told us there were twelve thousand pounds—in England. But she hadn't got a penny of them. There were plenty of explanations. It was nothing to do with M.—she had done everything she possibly could, from her end. Nor is it clear who is to blame, if " blame " one can call it. No doubt it doesn't look like that. Only it's damned hard on the party here. I could see Anne going hard and tight as she listened. We discussed the problem of the Friends, explaining to M. just how things look from our angle. We discussed the very pressing problem of legal aid for the prisoners. There are scarcely any Socialist lawyers who are not themselves in danger, and very few " Christian Socialists" who have the will or the courage to undertake the defence of the political prisoners, or even the immediate job of finding out where they are. When Anne's young man was in prison, she could not find out for eight days whether he was alive or dead. We discussed various other problems and difficulties.

Everyone left except Anne, for whom I made tea. We talked. She is younger than I am—quite a lot younger, but I had thought she was older. She makes me ashamed of the sheltered, lady-like life I have led. It's curious, one has always been led to expect the Viennese to be *gemütlich*—till one's sick of the word !—and elegant, gentle, perhaps too delicate, too spineless. And now I meet these people who are brave and tough, and with a kind of north-wind gaiety—something one has associated before with northerners. This woman has guts enough to make a Labour movement by herself. I take it that she is desperately tired ; she has been keeping up everyone's spirits ; she tells me stories of the fighting— and when the men's nerves broke, as men's nerves do, it was she who kept them together. Now perhaps she would like to be allowed to break a little. Having tea together was in some ways curiously like King's Norton—like the English Labour movement and my own *praxis*.

After she went to bed, I wrote till about 2 a.m. I tried pulling all the strings I have in the Labour movement, saying, " For God's sake send the

94

money ! " No doubt the letters will read hysterically when they get to England.

MARCH 4TH

Bad dreams, and waking tired—this disappointment about the money. In the morning I wrote diary, and then a young teacher turned up, about 11.30, eager and small and dark, with very dark deep-set eyes, heavily shadowed, and a twisted, charming smile. He spoke no English, so the conversation went slowly. I asked him first about what help was being given officially. He tells me that Caritas, the Catholic Aid Society, is busy, and the Government approves of help being given through it. However, it is entirely a Roman Catholic thing, run by nuns, priests, and the society women who always seem to be there in a Catholic country to do anything the dear Father tells them to do. But not everyone will take their money. He told me of the widow of one of the men from the Karl Marx Hof who was hanged. When offered help by the Innitzer fund, she said, " I don't want the Cardinal ; if my husband couldn't be saved by your money, I won't be." I think they would sooner starve. I have heard also of a woman who did let them take care of her starving children, who were then put into a convent !

95

It is a little difficult for us to realise the religious-political situation here. In England, and still more in Scotland, religion is a private thing, a contract between every individual man and woman and the universe. It may be mystic, or it may be mainly a matter of ethics ; in Scotland, at least it is something to be argued about. But we are shocked at the idea that it should be political. It very often is, in practice, but this is not admitted, and is scarcely a factor that can be counted upon. Most bishops, no doubt, are Conservatives, but a Socialist bishop would not be impossible in England.

But here it is all different. The Protestant Church scarcely counts, and the Catholic Church is a supporter of reaction—itself, in fact, *is* reaction. It is full of able politicians, who hold high religious offices, and who think in terms of politics. It is extremely awkward for a Catholic Church official—in this country at any rate—who happens also to be, in the English sense, a Christian. It is, for instance, extremely awkward for Cardinal Innitzer, who happens, as far as I can gather, to be one. He asks for religion, and they give him politics. I believe he is a good and kind and intelligent man ; I should think the present position was hell for him.

Take the position in the schools—this teacher whom I was talking to is a master at a school in one of the Gemeinde Hauser. He has a class of thirty-eight (not large, on English elementary-school standards). Of these, three were Protestants and ten *Konfessionslose*—anti-clericals. In the old days there was religious instruction twice a week, and these children did not go to it. Now the fathers, especially those in State employment, tramway-men, or men in gas or electricity works, for instance, have been told, by managers or others in authority, that " it will be better " if they send their children to religious instruction. Those who were very anxious, who were themselves in danger of any kind, did it at once, though some have still held out.

In his school, out of nine hundred children, there were about ninety atheists. During this last hard autumn and winter, some twenty or thirty children went back to confession—their parents were driven by bitter need to take help from the Church societies, which demanded their price. These were mostly the children of the *Lumpen-proletariat*—the unpolitical mass of the very poor. In general, he said, the more intelligent children came from the Gemeinde Hauser, where the politically conscious workers lived. In his class there were still five atheists with parents of this kind, men in the big, organised unions—or rather, men who were in these unions till their break-up. Even they will probably have to compromise, to give at least lip-service, though the heart is unchanged. And how bad this may be for children !

Since Christmas, there has been a new Dollfuss regulation, ordering schools to begin the morning with prayers. Up to now, some of the teachers have had nothing to do with it, and some of the children have refused to attend too. Now most of the children come, but some of them don't understand at all, and some of them rag the prayers. Very few children are religious in any real sense. The Catholic teaching is that the Bible doesn't matter, but one must go to church ; this, I suppose, must always seem very shocking to anyone with a Protestant background, although when one thinks of the Mass as a kind of magic ceremony, it is reasonable enough. But Cardinal Innitzer, for instance, was anti-political just because he saw that politics destroy religion when the same body of people try to carry on both activities. For they are in deadly enmity. He, for instance, did not want these irreligious school prayers, but the Dollfuss Government and the politicians in his own Church were too much for him.

All this gives one a much clearer idea of the Russian situation. It would have been unreasonable and cruel of any Government to stop the practice of personal religion as we are apt to think of it in Scotland, and so we censure the Soviet Government —some of us—not realising that the kind of religion which it was destroying was essentially political, just as this is. If there is ever (as please God there will be, say the Protestant Socialists) another Socialist Government in Vienna, they will take violent measures against the Catholic Church, and, if we have any kind of understanding, we shall not deny their right to do so. I am inclined to think that Protestantism—at any rate ours in Scotland, where we let no man, nor even the Kirk Session, come between us and our concept of the universe—is essentially equalitarian and therefore Social Democrat, though it may be too individualist to allow of Communism. But once you get an ordered Church with a hierarchy, and a hierarchy who through their magic-giving office can deny or delay or hasten the contact between man and his at-one-ment, then immediately you have sympathy with other forms of hierarchy, especially those of the State; the Church necessarily joins hands with the monarchy and Conservatism.

There are more plans for the schools by the Government. My friend knew of ninety teachers who had been dismissed. But at present no one can say what the next step will be.

I asked him about himself. He was not in danger, at least not immediately, but his mother was a well-known party official. She has been in prison since the 15th of the month. He cannot see her; they can only write post-cards to one another, saying, " I am quite well," or something like that. He can bring her clean linen, but when he asks about her the prison officials are bloody to him. Poor little man, with those dark soft eyes, how on earth can anyone find it in their hearts to bully him ! In his district there were five Socialist municipal councillors; all but one are in prison, and no one has been allowed to speak to them.

I talked to him a little about politics. Clearly he knows nothing about the part of his own party which is still alive, and I did not know how much I could tell him. He showed me a long list of names and addresses—a few of them were the same which I had got last time from Mrs. T., and he was very glad to hear that they had got help. I asked him to make me a list of those who needed legal advice most desperately. He had hoped to turn over all his lists to me, but now he kept one back ; it is dangerous for him to have these lists in his pocket—supposing the police came and searched . . . Obviously we *Ausländer* must act as intermediaries between all these people with lists and the body which is giving out the money. When it comes. . . .

We had lunch, and I tried to cheer him up a little. He carried on a long political discussion with me in a rapid whisper that I could scarcely follow. Now and then I picked up the thread of it, but then I would lose it again. He knows something of the personnel of the English movement, and wanted to know about the Left-wingers. I tried to explain the Socialist League. He told me that out of his class of thirty-eight only three were passed by the doctor as perfectly sound ; the others all had something wrong. The best were from the Gemeinde Hauser. But they were mostly born in a bad time—a time of hunger and infinite depression ; they showed it physically.

He told me that the Heimwehr get five Austrian Schillings a week, and that men are joining now for that. He talked with the greatest affection about the children in his school. He told of people who had got no help yet, and to whom none could safely come—men whose houses were being watched, for instance. I gave him 100 Schillings, asking him, when possible, to say it came from English party comrades. I felt I was screening Transport House from the sad and piercing scrutiny of those brown eyes.

After that I took him over to Sam's, and he had a talk with Janet, who was charming to him. I suppose she is the sort of woman who isn't particularly charming in drawing-rooms ; she reserves it for people like this. We got his address, and then had to dash off. I took some necessary documents with me ; one mustn't wave these about, so I stuffed them into a pocket. Thank goodness I have a solid skirt—and one whose pocket holds a lot without bulging too much. Mary has been carrying hers mostly in her knickers. One begins to distrust the ordinary bag which does for lip-sticks and that kind of thing.

I keep on hearing of the different kinds of relief which are going about—all the various organisations which are trying to get at the workers. Nazi relief, Czech relief, various kinds of official relief. Some people say Russian relief, but I rather doubt it.

Now we went to a hotel and saw Sir Philip Gibbs, to whom Sam was talking—a nice, gentle, bothered

Liberal, wanting to do the right thing but not sure
what it was. Being talked to by so many people that
he must have lost any possibility of coming to
an independent decision. At the same time he
must have learnt to put out a kind of resilient
defence against propaganda. We three did our best
with our point of view, and he was very nice to
us.

Back at the hotel, M. turned up, having spent a
profitable day, like the hosts of Midian, prowling
and prowling around, and getting at points of view.
The evening before, I had tried to explain her to
Anne. But it is very hard for any foreigner to understand the type of Englishwoman, who, like M., does
not work through any political party, but yet has
contact—contact of a kind which the professional
politician only too often loses. In a Catholic country
there is nothing between the party worker and the
church-lady who slums, and possibly the same kind
of thing is true of every country where politics is
taken really seriously—either you are in the party or
you do not have contact. But in England, as I keep on
feeling more and more strongly, politics are not taken
seriously, even now. Up to a few years ago, it was
definitely a game, where—as in other English sports
—you shook hands with your opponents first. And
kept the gloves on. Some people will say this was a
good thing. Conceivably it was a necessary psycho-
logical basis for democracy as conceived by our
immediate ancestors and generally by ourselves.

At any rate, it produced the type of the upper middle-class intelligent woman, too serious-minded to enter the male game of politics—the woman who runs the clinics and organisations and clubs which in other countries are bound up with politics and/ or religion, but not yet in England. Such women claim for themselves an objectivity—*au-dessus de la mêlée*—which is probably false, for I cannot believe that any of us are really objective, and I can quite see how Anne, for instance, entirely fails to find a correct and comfortable standpoint from which she can talk with M. They will have, I take it, to arrive at this through personal contact. I am, of course, much more like M. than I am like Anne, or any of the party people, but I am not sure how much this is clear to them.

M., like the rest of us, is terribly bothered about the situation, and the fact that there is no money. She is going to write back to those in high places, whom she herself saw—I think it puzzles Anne that Transport House should have had anything to do with an envoy who is not officially a comrade ! That's English democracy, of course. We are all writing back. C. will take the letters to-morrow.

After M. went, Anne and her young man came and typed a letter here, and I went off to see the correspondent of that paper generally recognised as supreme in England, the *Ponderous Press*. I took with me a sheaf of our news. He was at work when I got there, so I talked with his sister, pleasantly enough, mostly of English news. When he came out, I tried to put it to him that the line which the *Ponderous Press* is taking is not helpful. They may take the official view that Dollfuss is to be supported, but his best chance of success (or rather the " Christian Socialists' " best chance of success, for I'm sure Dollfuss himself is finished) is to behave decently now. If the present Government realises that foreign opinion will not support it unless it acts with moderation, it is more likely to do so, and thus, of course, strengthen its own hand against the German Nazis. At present the workers are going over to the Nazis, and they will continue to do so, in spite of the pretty posters about brotherhood and forgiveness, unless the present people actually do stop this wholesale beating and imprisoning and outlawing. I doubt whether they will ever accept Dollfuss again—he had better go to America and become a professor—but they might accept a "Christian Socialist" Government of the Left, supported by Innitzer. That seems for the moment the best for Europe, and we can only see round one corner at a time. If they realise that we in England disapprove of their present methods, they are likely to stop them, and the Left-wing "Christian Socialists" will have the credit for this, as against Fey and Starhemberg. And the best way of showing that England disapproves is through the semi-official *Ponderous Press*.

I tried to explain all this to the correspondent, instancing what the *Ponderous Press* has done in the past—including the quite recent past—in the interests of European decency. I have known the correspondent since he was an inky small boy, and this made it no easier. Obviously he looks on me as one of these interfering Bolshie women, but at the same time he realises that I do represent some intangible Thing or Opinion. He tells me that of course in civil war—he will talk about it as The Revolt, like a preparatory-school history book—one expects Severities. I tell him that of course I am not complaining of this, that, and the other, but of the other, that, and this. He says we must have Perspective. I answer that, as one of the people who are likely to be beaten up or hung in an English civil war (or Revolt), I am hoping that he will try to get it into people's heads that some things are Not Done. In a way, I suppose, I am trying to be a Gladstonian Liberal, an attitude which was all very well in the time of England's prosperity when we could tick off the dirty foreigners. But if anyone in England can still adopt this Gladstonian tone, and carry it off successfully, it is the *Ponderous Press*. He says, inevitably, that stories of the fighting are no longer news, and that he wants something up to date. I explain that the difficulty is one can't see people the moment they've been beaten, and that the news is as fresh as it can be. I also explain that the probability is that they are doing the same kind of thing in the provinces now as they did in Vienna a week ago. He says he will think it over, and discuss matters with the Legation. Let's hope something has come of it.

From there to Lass—late, and hungry. On the way I had a talk with a jolly woman, who showed me the street I wanted—goodness knows who she was, probably the wife of a shop-keeper, but very friendly, and distinctly upset by recent events. Lass's hostess gave me delicious salad, with lumps of something nice in it, and cheese and fruit, and I discussed things with her. The question is, How much of the little money I and the few others have is to be spent on actual relief?—it may be wanted much more for other things, especially if most of the T.U. money is to go on direct relief, as seems possible.

MARCH 5TH : MORNING

Coming home I found Anne and I., another eminent woman Socialist. Anne went across to Sam's, and I made tea for I., and helped her to look out trains in the time-table. She was incredibly kind and nice, looking at me with a tired benevolence from behind her spectacles, but she was a little Victorian over her handling of the time-table ; it made me feel almost practical. She had cropped hair, and she was desperately tired and probably ill. She reminded me rather of Beatrice Webb. I can imagine, say, some Scandinavian Socialist helping Beatrice Webb to look up trains, after a *débâcle* in England. . . .

Now I must type out some lists of names, and I must try and write to King's Norton. One thing about all this—it is definitely slimming. I could comfortably take two inches off the belt of my skirt !

MARCH 5TH : AFTERNOON

I had just finished my lists when M. turned up, and, gradually, the others. Whether it's wise for us to lunch in large—and, I should have thought, rather conspicuous—parties, is another matter. At least it doesn't look awfully like conspiracy. There was much talk. M. had been to the Legation, and seen the authorities there. She discussed the official view ; we put forward ours ; she was being very impartial—very English. Perhaps very sensible, but suddenly Anne, who had been silent, said, in a low, thick voice, " I feel like an Armenian among you." She was blushing then, and tears stood in her eyes, which were never shed.

It recalled the rest of us out of our hypothetical English politics to the actual present here, where real

107

people are really being killed and tortured. And yet we were all out of it, protected by our passports and our jobs in England, and she was in it, defended only by her own wits and courage ; it was all very well talking politics, but our immediate job was to give her solidarity—if we could not do that we were no good as Socialists. It was *praxis* in personal relationships. I do not know how well we succeeded.

Evert had been away over the frontier ; the jolly, solid *Mädchen* on our floor seemed rather upset when he didn't come back—normally I am told all about him as soon as I come in : " Der Herr Doktor ist in dem Klosett . . ."—so I smiled and said I understood he had gone for a long walk with a lady (which was, indeed, true). He and the lady, who looks jolly and competent, now came in to lunch. He avoided our rather conspicuous party, but after lunch told Sam that he was now probably suspect. He and the lady had walked along a curiously unguarded piece of frontier, and over into —— where they had visited the Arbeiterheim, which was full of Schutzbundlers. He was still under the influence of that heroic impression of ordinary men transformed, as they were, by what had happened. The only awful thing was that they could get no word of their wives and children—if only they could know that they weren't starving at home, it would have been all right for them. And Evert, worse luck, couldn't truthfully say that the comrades from England were looking after them all ! These men had been brave and honest ; they had all been very near death ; they still had the bloom of it upon them ; they were heroes, at least for Evert, only—there was one traitor. He had not been found yet, but the head of the home had opened all the letters (which Evert was taking back) so as to trace him. One woman, coming back with letters, had been caught at the frontier and searched. Evert was uncertain whether he ought to take back letters, but finally decided to, as an Englishman with a passport. They had wanted him to go and see Deutsch and try to persuade him about a certain course of action, but he refused—fortunately as it turned out. On the way back, his and his friend's passports were carefully scrutinised, but that was all. However, he may easily be being followed. He was a good deal worried, as he doesn't want to be turned out, or to involve others. He laid various plans for to-morrow, to see the Press Bureau, the Legation, etc., and to establish himself as much as possible. After all, this was part of his job as a good journalist ; he has to see every side of things. Being a journalist ought to clear him, as being a writer ought to clear me. By the way, I have found some-one who is going to translate some of my books into German ; that will be rather fun.

MARCH 6TH

I am writing between one and two in the afternoon, waiting, either till Evert comes back (he was due back at twelve), or till someone comes to whom, in the event of Evert being in any way kept, I was to give a message. So far, nothing. I did not finish last night, because by two in the morning I was excessively tired and felt as though I had a slight temperature. To-day I'm all right, but ridiculously white.

I went, in the afternoon, to Y's office, where I met a Social Democrat *Fürsorgerin*. I had hoped to go round to places with her, but she was not free ; we arranged a meeting for Wednesday. This is the worst of not being able to telephone freely—one wastes time and shoe-leather. Her district is not one of the bad ones—there was no fighting. But there are some cases of need arising out of the recent events. She says she sends people to the Soziale-Hilfe (the official fund), but they won't go. They are afraid. Or else they refuse on other grounds. The people who run the Soziale-Hilfe, she says, are many of them good sort of people, not necessarily even Catholics, but they are " ladies." People won't talk to them. I don't think the Soziale-Hilfe people in her district are doing political or religious propaganda, except, to some extent, implicitly ; but people just don't trust them. It's inevitable. I asked about other kinds of help—mentioned the Quakers. She said she was afraid of them—afraid, that is, that the lists of names which she sent there might not be safe. Equally, people wouldn't go to the Singer-Strasse, the Quaker centre, on the same grounds. There are constant rumours that a Government commissar may be put into the Quaker office " to superintend." This may be quite baseless, but it is enough to frighten people. I told this woman that if she liked to make two sorts of lists—one " safe," the other " dangerous "—and give them to me, I would hand the safe names to the Quakers, and arrange about the others. This seems to be rather up to me to do, and it is purely humanitarian work ; my conscience doesn't bother me. We arranged to meet again, preferably with someone who can translate—she has no English, and my German is still very slow and with bad gaps—but she asked me to wait in the office for a few minutes, so as not to leave with her.

I then walked over to Lass's—on my way looking in at shop windows in the luxury streets. They have the most fascinating embroidered jerseys, just what I like best, and I am trying to make up my mind whether I can decently get one—since on the one hand if I do I can leave both my own rather aged woollies behind here (clothes are wanted badly for some families), and I would get something that would go with the light coat and skirt which I simply must get this spring—I'd meant to last spring, but royalties didn't run to it !—and, on the other hand, it would be a pound or so which otherwise would go to Floridsdorf. . . . I haven't squared my conscience yet, but they're lovely jerseys !

I handed over my lists to Lass, much to the indignation of Jake, who really hates me for wasting his mother's time which ought to be devoted to him ! She is hard at it still. Then I handed in my other list to the Friends, who now seem very busy, with a constant stream of people coming in and out. Back to Ian's flat, where the usual crowd had collected. I gave them chocolate, which I'd bought to soothe myself about the jerseys ! Ian said I was to meet two journalists that evening, so, as it was now about seven, I went back and started changing into a tidy frock.

(Evert has just rung up—he was kept, but not officially. So far no word of the man for whom the message in my pocket is to go.)

I had washed and put on thin silk stockings, and a silk petticoat, and was just brushing my hair, when the telephone-bell rang. It was Janet, ringing up to ask if I knew where Ian was—I didn't, and Evert didn't. She seemed a little agitated, and explained that " an extraordinary phenomenon is occurring," and that Ian must be stopped before he got back to the flat. The only thing to do, plainly, was to patrol the street and catch him. I scrambled into my day-clothes again, took the papers I had put into my passport out, and locked them up—there was

nothing obviously incriminating ; Evert had burned
all his possibly incriminating documents. Then I
hurried across the town to Ian's, running where it
didn't look too silly. There I found Janet, who
showed me the quite obvious plain-clothes-man
walking up and down, and told me to take on till
8.15. Ian was due back any time. The rest were in
the café. Mary had taken the other end of the
road. I waited outside, my feet very cold in the silk
stockings (which went badly with my coat and
skirt), trying to look like a young woman waiting
for her boy-friend. Unfortunately I am short-
sighted, and, to see across the street, I have to wear
horn spectacles, which make me look definitely odd.
Occasionally I glanced at my Baedeker, and
pretended to be a tourist, or else I tried to look just
mildly cross. Actually I felt extremely uncomfortable ; it was all worse than, for instance, the murder
game, which anyhow terrifies me ! This is the kind
of thing I'm no good at ; I got nerves, kept on thinking that Ian would come back in a taxi . . . or
disguised as an old lady . . . or wearing a kilt. . . . I
didn't suppose anything much would happen to
him, even if he was arrested, but I was afraid for the
others. I didn't even know how much afraid I had
to be. Probably I looked far more suspicious myself
than the plain-clothes man did ! I kept on wondering
what M., now writing an official letter back, still
under the spell of English legality, would think of it.
By and bye, K. came hurrying past me, saying, " Go

in ! " I went in, and they were nice, but laughing at me for looking so obvious and so worried. K., who had often " played with her neck," thought it all rather funny.

We sat in the café for a time, and then K. began to worry too ; her brother came back, very pale, black under the eyes, jumpy. No one could think where Ian was—he ought to have been back. And, if he had been caught, what would he have on him ? By and bye I was told to go out again, and this time to take the other end of the road. I walked along, looking as innocent as I could—but no doubt suspicious enough !—and was challenged by a Heimwehr sentry ; however, as I didn't understand what he said, I just walked on. Evert was at the far end, all thrilled ; rumour had it that the house was surrounded by spies and police. Actually there were two. I waited for a bit, and K. came up, laughing, and took me by the arm and shook me into laughing too. Evert came back, and said that Ian had been stopped, and now Janet was going to the house to see that everything was all right. It was possible that the police were waiting " for a young man of about eighteen with a large hat "—if I saw him, would I stop him ? Extremely nervously, I said I would, long‐ing to be back in South Kensington or North Oxford ! And by and bye, along came a young man of about eighteen, but without a hat. I became a sleuth-hound. He looked cautiously down the street, as though he wasn't sure where to go, so I thought it was worth a chance and addressed him in English (which I had been told the right young man understood). He answered, and I had the difficult job of trying to find out whether he was Ian's friend. I had just become convinced that he wasn't, and that he probably thought I was trying to get off with him, when Evert turned up, and I disentangled myself with infinite clumsiness, realising, with shame, that I am not made for a life of—say, crime. In fact, Evert and I were both in fits of giggles when K. and her brother met us, and sobered us slightly by telling us what to do or say if they were arrested.

We came back to the hotel, Evert enjoying himself —for, after all, to few of us is it given at (hush !) twenty-three, to be engaged in these kind of activities—I only wishing I were back with the nice legal English Labour Party. In fact, as we went up in the lift, I was nearly crying with anxiety. I changed, trying to brace up to meet the journalists, and we had dinner—it was now past nine. We both felt we'd like something lightish, like eggs, and asked the Herr Ober, for something really original in the way of eggs. After deep thought, he suggested an omelette. So we compromised disgustedly on *Pariser Schnitzel* and an *Achtel Gespritzten* each. After the darkness and tension of the street, this was a curious relaxation. Both of us, our glorious sinews loosened, began to talk extremely freely to one another about ourselves, which was rather comforting.

Then came the journalists, the correspondents of
two big American papers, whom I shall call Tweedledum—he was large and fair and kindly—and
Tweedledee, who was comparatively small and dark,
and a superb actor and story-teller. They both
started off by assuming that I was an innocent
author, and trying to convince me that the Socialists
really were rather fine people. So that was all right.
Evert stayed—it was just as well, if he was suspected,
to be into touch with senior members of his profession—and soon got into an extremely grim and
bluggy conversation with Tweedledum about the
number of bodies he had seen on the first day of the
fighting. Both the correspondents were very sympathetic, and we began to discuss ways and means.
During dinner, Mary had brought in our documents
about things which had been happening both here
and in the provinces ; she was being rather solemn
and secret too, and we passed the stuff across the
table as though it would explode !

They all three began talking about the fighting in
the first week—war stories—and Tweedledee began
a horrid one about a woman waiting to hear whether
her husband was hung. He told it brilliantly, and I
nearly screamed, my nerves were all frayed by now.
Evert had gone to telephone, for Ian had said he
would be here by 10.30, and now it was eleven. We
didn't know whether to tell these two what had
happened ; there was no news by telephone, and
everyone was talking horrors—and then Ian walked

in, smiling and cool, and Highland as ever, and I was so relieved I nearly fell on his neck—or fainted. I think he must have been much flattered at the idea of half the Englishwomen in Vienna guarding his room against the *Kriminalbeamter* ! They all went on telling stories, and discussing ways of getting them over—the two Americans talked of revolutions and terrors they had been in, compared with which this was a happy day at Brighton, but still they were both on the right side—as anyone must be who has been about the place during the last few weeks. They emphasised, what I'd heard already, that the Socialists had been so desperately gentlemanly all through, that they had given—and expected—fair play. We all knew that they had stores of dynamite, which they hadn't used for fear of blowing up innocent people. Now Tweedledum told us of a machine-gunner who was not allowed by his captain to enfilade the soldiers who were taking up position against them, because the soldiers had not yet fired, and were conceivably not going to, nor was he allowed to fire at a regiment which was firing at another house. It might well have been England. And it *is* because of this concept of fair play that they are all so horrified at howitzers having been used against them—contrary to the rules of the game.

We discussed what was going to happen to the prisoners, and Tweedledee said that what shocked him so much was seeing Weber, the man who had planned so many of the Gemeinde Hauser, who had given sun and light and space to play and be happy in to so many thousands of people, now shut up in a little cell, pacing backwards and forwards like a beast. I suppose they will delay the trials for some time, but one wonders what is going to happen then. The whole position about legal aid is pretty bad, as there are hardly any lawyers left to defend the thousands of prisoners.

The correspondents suggested a very good contact for us, which Ian proceeded to make at once, and then they went off, very friendlily. I made tea for Evert, and, just as I'd poured out, Anne came back. She was extraordinarily gay, and told us funny stories about the various respectable Socialist leaders. She is the kind of person who should have survival value ; civilisation needs her.

I slept rather badly, with disquieting dreams ; even when everything has turned out all right, this isn't good for one. In the morning, after a telephone call or two, I went round to Ian's flat. He had been worrying a good deal, trying to stop all his friends coming, who might be in danger if they did ; he had been doing that since early in the morning, and now he had gone out to go on doing it. I found Gert's sister mending a chair ; she is the sort of person who is good for one if one's feeling rather demoralised— she can suggest jobs which need doing and which involve a certain amount of risk, perhaps more. She can always be called upon for anything. And is !

Then I went off into one of the districts with Janet. We went to an oldish tenement house in a side-street, and up the stairs. On the third floor we came to a two-roomed flat, and a woman opened the door a few inches and stared at us. Janet explained, in a whisper, that we were all right, and we went in. Again came the hand-clasp and the whispered *Freundschaft*. In the back room there was a dilapidated-looking bed, a sewing-machine, an aquarium full of little fishes, and a table with bits of leather cut out and lying on it. By the table was the shoemaker, a small, dark-eyed man, typically Viennese, with a round head, and black hair sticking up. One eye was partly closed, and looked sore. In his right hand he held his shoemaker's awl ; that hand had a silver wedding-ring, engraved with a date and some words, and across the back of it was a scar, newly skinned over. Beside him was his wife, a plain, worried woman, badly dressed, and in the other room, or fidgeting about nervously between them, was the dark-eyed, pale-faced boy, his son. They spoke in whispers, and often he gesticulated, at me or Janet, acting what had happened, sometimes catching Janet by one arm.

The little man was a shoemaker, working for a wholesale firm. On the Monday of the bad week, he was called up by his friend—this friend had now been arrested for the second time. Three hundred were fetched on the Monday, by word of mouth, as support troops for the Schutzbund. He was up with

the machine guns in the attics of a certain house.
On the Monday night they started shelling, and a
dud shell came crashing in. They thought then it was
time to change their position, and hoped to be able
to get out and away with their machine guns, and
possibly get behind the howitzers and attack them
from there. They went down into the cellars, with
their machine guns and other stuff, after considerable
difficulties. They knew already of the way out—
through the network of sewers and air passages that
go under the city.

He and eight others—he didn't know what had
happened to the rest—got into the air-shaft above
the sewer. For a time they took the weapons with
them, then it narrowed till they had to go on all
fours, and there they left the stuff. By and bye it
widened out, and they could stand. They came to a
place with a dynamo and a great fan. This was all
at midnight of Monday. They had one pocket-torch
among them.

They came to an outlet at the end of the air-shaft,
with a man-hole. Very cautiously they lifted the lid
of the man-hole ; they thought they knew where
they were, but were not sure. It opened into a
cylindrical chamber, with a glass top, several yards
above them. Here there were pipes and wires, and,
in one corner, a pole, up which one of them climbed,
to see whether it was safe for them to try and get out.
But, when he came to the glass top and looked out,
he could see that the courtyard was already no good ;

there were police there, searching. So the nine men went back along the air-shaft to the place below the house from which they had started, where the central heating was, and electric fans, and here they found two candles. They lighted the candles, and tried to find another way to get their machine guns out. They thought they knew of one ; it should have been the main underground passage to a school, where they could have escaped ; but, half-way along it, they came to a heap of bricks, and they couldn't anyhow get past. They thought at first it was something to do with rebuilding, but then they realised that all this must be the result of the bombardment and the crashing down of walls.

So now they went back to the central-heating chamber, and made up their minds that there was nothing to be done but destroy their weapons so that they should at least never come into the hands of their enemies. They turned the water of the central-heating pipes on to the rifles, to rust them up, and, as for the machine guns, they stood them in a corner and threw hand grenades at them, and so destroyed them. They heard firing going on, but they did not know what was happening, only the plaster kept raining down on their heads, shaken loose by the bursting of the shells, and they thought that soon the whole house would fall in on them.

Now it was just nine on Tuesday morning—they had eaten last at mid-day on Monday. The little shoemaker had seen a clock in the central-heating chamber, just by the candles. And the nine men were down there, and a police inspector came—with police and Heimwehr, young and old—and said, " Hands up." And, when the nine men put up their hands, the police and the Heimwehr men began to hit them with rifle butts, and when they were driven up out of the cellar, and marched out into the street, still they hit them with rifle butts. The worst were the quite young police and Heimwehr. People at each side of the street ran to their windows, crying out in horror and disgust, " *O weh !* " So the police pointed their rifles at the windows, and called out that they would shoot if there was any noise.

It had been said in the party, before all this, that the party had two sorts of weapons, the real weapons, and the spiritual—the *geistige Waffen*. So now, when the police and Heimwehr hit them, they would say, " *Da haben Sie geistige Waffen !* " (" There's your spiritual weapons ! "). And they called them *Rote Hunde* (Red dogs), and *Kellerratten* (sewer rats)— " sewer rats that need hanging." And so they were taken to the police-station. Mostly they had rifle barrels at their temples ; the little shoemaker had his eye hurt that way—though not so very badly, it wasn't right before. Even before this, he was an ugly little proletarian with a bad eye, not tall or noble-looking. He did not complain about this, but one man had the skin and flesh by his eye so torn that the eye-ball dropped out on to his cheek.

Well then, they were taken from the *Wachstube* to the Commissariat, the central police-station, where they were not hurt, not beaten anyhow. But they were in the courtyard there when someone fired from a house which overlooked it, and a policeman was hit. The police began to fire back, and at last got the man who had fired, and brought him in and beat him so that four men had to carry him in. He was thrown into a cell—the little shoemaker saw all this—and covered with a cloth on the ground, and then they beat at him with their rifle butts, sometimes hitting him, and sometimes hitting the ground or the walls, so that when they came out their rifle butts were splintered. But, whether the man lived or died, the little shoemaker did not know.

From there they were sent to barracks, and there they were all put into a room with other prisoners, men, women, and children together, and they had nothing to eat until Thursday. Police officers came and looked at them, for it had been reported that these nine were " the most dangerous men from ——." And all Wednesday and Thursday the prisoners stayed there, talking to one another, telling one another their stories.

Most of them had been beaten up, at any rate most of the men who had been caught or suspected with weapons. More people were wounded by the Heimwehr and police beatings than ever by shells or rifle fire. The worst were taken to hospital, or passed on from one prison to another, so that they should not come out till the marks were more or less healed. Inevitably, the men were hit on the genitals.

Their money had been taken from them at the police-station, and anything else they had on them. When they left, some of them asked for it back. But that was no good. Someone would say, " What are you asking for ? " " One Schilling, forty Groschen." And bang would come the smack on the face that was the only answer. " What are you asking for ? " " My knife." And the smack on the face again. There was a woman who was taken with fifty Schillings on her, with which she had been going to repay a loan. But, when she asked for it back, all she got was filthy words. No one got anything back from the police-station.

Such things the prisoners told one another, while they waited, dead-hungry, and thirsty, for to get to the water-tap under which they drank, for there was no cup, each had to go with a Heimwehr bayonet at his or her neck. There had been a kind of V.A.D. organisation attached to the Schutzbund—the Samaritaines. One of these girls, a twenty-year-old Jewess, had been arrested. She wanted to help with the hurt men, but they wouldn't let her. Her hair had been torn off the back of her head, and her skin with it, so that she had a festering wound there. They called her *Rote Hure* (Red prostitute), *Jüdische Hure* ; they had shoved fingers up her nose, and torn the nostrils right up ; they had torn her ear-lobes.

I think the little shoemaker minded that as much as anything.

By and bye an army officer came in, and this man plucked up courage to ask him whether they could smoke, because they were so hungry. The officer hadn't known ; he gave the shoemaker twenty cigarettes, and said he would see that they got food. Perhaps it was because there were children among the prisoners who had not eaten either. Several officers came in, and they brought food, which they paid for themselves—he saw them take out the money and pay. So, after that, they had enough to eat.

And on Friday they were beckoned out one by one, and their evidence was taken. They were asked how they got into the building. The shoemaker said he had gone out to buy more leather, and he got into the crowd and was carried away. And they believed him, and on the Monday they let him go. And he came back to his wife.

While they were in the barracks, they wanted to write home, even though their letters would be censored, but none of them had any money, not a Groschen, so not one letter could be sent back to tell their wives and children. But, as men and women were let go free, they arranged about the letters. There was a *pissoir*, with an opening—a barred window—through into the street. And the men using this could shove their letters through quickly in the moment when the guard had his back turned. This way the shoemaker's wife found out on Saturday morning what had happened to her husband ; she knew nothing till then.

One of the wives had been let out, and wrote back to her husband. She said, " You will die of shock when you come home. We are nothing but beggars (*total bettelarm*). . . . The Heimwehr have been through the house ; they have torn the mattresses to pieces ; they have broken everything. There is even no under-clothing left, except what you have got on you."

For all this time the Heimwehr were searching for weapons. And they searched with ruthless thoroughness. They looked for weapons with their bayonets, digging them through furniture and everything. That was what they went back to. Some didn't go back. He doesn't know what happened to the Jewess ; she was taken away on the Friday.

Of the nine men, four have already been re-arrested. There is constant gossip going round ; he does not know when it will reach him. But already they are talking about him in the building—" Why were the others re-arrested and not him ? " Here, his wife joined in, and said that she hardly dared open her door or speak to a soul. If they come for him—— He says he dare not face it again.

He was hit in the back, and is still passing blood with his urine ; he cannot sit down comfortably. The doctor says it is a contusion of the kidneys. The hand ? It was stamped upon by a police boot. They would not let him bring back his cap, it was so stuck with blood. He cannot sleep.

Janet gave them some money, from the comrades. I gave him some of the stuff I have for sleeping. I hope he may get one or two good nights. Then, if they come, he may have got back the nerve he must have had on the Monday when he was first called up. We whispered again the word *Freundschaft*. And he smiled sweetly and ironically, and we left him cutting out the leather shapes for the wholesale shop, but never sitting down, because that hurt so much.

Between one and two, I wrote my diary, and waited for the man to come for whom I had the message. But he never came. We do not know at all what has happened to him, or whether he is safe. We shall not know for days.

At half past two, V. came for me, and we set out together. She was very much worried at the lack of money ; Schutzbundlers had come to her for help to get away, but she couldn't do anything for lack of money. I said I could let her have a couple of hundred, which is all she needs at the moment, but, oh, God, why doesn't Transport House do something ! We walked through several streets to a small flower-shop, where we picked up the proprietress, who looked very smart in a short fur coat and a little hat and half veil over sleek face and hair. One wouldn't have expected her to be a sound party woman. The two of them talked party stuff hard, I think mostly about illegal publishing activities, but I was getting extremely sleepy, and my German kept on fading out. We took a train, which by and bye dropped us outside the Karl Marx Hof. It was astonishing enough to come out of the station in face of this superb building, with its soft red cliff of frontage pierced by low arches, and surmounted by blunt, square towers. It was built from 1927 to 1930, and houses 15,000 people. V. looked at it, and said, " We used to be so proud of this." I said, " You have more reason to be proud of it now."

We passed under one of those low, generously wide arches, and out into the three-sided court, flooded with sunshine, and brilliant sunshine on the long western cliff and the shining women that stand on the corner-stones of the arches. It was extraordinarily beautiful, and for me, at least, the occasional spatterings of bullet-marks made no difference to the thing as a whole. Here we passed an old man arguing with two girls, saying that he would not go home and get arrested again. He wasn't going to be called a *Roter Hund* again ! " Take care how you make notes in sight of the Heimwehr ! " said V. And then we went on round the Hof, and came at last to the main gate of the enclosed square, which had been shelled. The tower was badly smashed, though it could be repaired—if anyone was going to. It was barred across, and there was a sentry, but we got past, saying we had people to see.

We found our man, in a two-roomed flat that opened on to a balcony full of sunlight, though how much longer will he be able to stay there? They were a husband and wife—the husband a *Konfessionslose*, the wife a Catholic (which accounted for the text embroidered on a wall-hanging), but in full sympathy. The man was very friendly, though at first nervous. He was a fair-skinned, brown-eyed man, with a shock of light hair—a German type. The flower proprietress introduced us. They all seemed to know her there—so she must have some standing in the party. I had begun to realise, from the way those two women talked, how *shocked* the party people are by the shelling of the buildings. I can't help feeling that, once civil war had started, the shelling was probably inevitable, and not so bad as various other things which have happened. But it must have been very shocking and unexpected at the time.

The man began to tell us about the fighting, the usual story of disorganisation and bad communications. There had been fighting on Monday night. But there was nothing on Tuesday morning from 7 to 10 a.m., when the howitzers opened fire on them for an hour. Then everyone went indoors, and the great door was locked. But a tramway-man gave the soldiers the key, and they came and searched, shouting at every door, " Come out, or we will shoot." So everyone went out—men, women, and children.

Every man who was suspected of bearing arms was separated from the rest by the soldiers. And then the Heimwehr men came and hunted again for Schutz- bundlers, and everyone was terrified of being shot. A number of people were killed and wounded, including two women in one flat. Now all the men in the Karl Marx Hof were arrested—first the suspects, then the others. Some were sent home at once, and it was all right for them. But others were kept in prison for several days. The out-of-work have of course lost their cards and their insurance ; I don't think anyone knows what is to happen to them ultimately.

The men were marched to the police-station, twenty minutes away, always with their hands up. There were old men among them but if they began to drop their hands they were jabbed in the armpits with bayonets. At the police-station they were hand- cuffed, and some were knocked about.

This man and his brother had both been betrayed by a neighbour, who said they were Socialist, but were let out. The brother, though, is in prison again—his name was given as a Schutzbundler by a man who was beaten till he gave some names. The first time, this man was put into a cell with a man whom he knew to have no political views, but who had a black eye and fainted three times. He was taken to hospital, and there they found that the bones of his hand were broken too. Another man who was in this cell was the man who made the arms for the

Schutzbund, and he was beaten so that he couldn't stand. This man is now in the military prison ; his wife and child have committed suicide.

Whenever they were questioned, they were beaten, though this man got off better than some. There was a room where ten or fifteen men always waited to do the beating. A party official was beaten up and taken to the police hospital. After the questioning, at which I don't think he was systematically beaten, he was put in a four-man-cell, now holding twenty-four, including those who had been badly beaten. He was there for twenty-four hours. But, in the provincial court, he said, he was all right : there were Socialists there !

He spoke of various happenings—of a family of father and four sons, where weapons were found and one son bayoneted in the leg ; of how the police stopped the Heimwehr from looting, and even took away their weapons. He has a young brother of fourteen, now in the children's hospital " for his nerves." He spoke also of the re-arresting. For a week the police-van didn't come. Then, yesterday and the day before, it did come, and took away eleven men. The day before yesterday, one of the men was visited by his girl, who saw the marks of beating on him, and our friend saw the girl, who told him about it, yesterday. This is the nearest evidence one can get to the beatings, which are undoubtedly going on now—not in every district certainly, but wherever there was fighting. He also told us how yesterday they had again raided for arms in the kindergarten.

The man himself is a tailor, but has not had work for some time. He had a temporary job as builder before all this, with a State building of some kind. But now the State only takes on Vaterländische Front men and " Christian Socialists," so he is out of that job. And anyway, I suppose they will now go in for economies over building !

We said good-bye and *Freundschaft*—in a whisper. And so back, passing one or two other of those beautiful buildings. Now it was evening. I wrote, and Janet and Mary came in, both very much worried over a Schutzbundler who has managed to give himself away to the police by telephoning to his wife—they have to find him a lodging to-night. I left them and Ian settling that, while Evert and I went to G., and walked with him to his office, where he settles down for an hour's night-work. He was very cheering in a way, making it seem all part of life—as it must be to him after all these years of newspaper work. Strupye, the charming mongrel, bounded happily through the night, dragging him along or pulling him back. And now again it is nearly one in the morning, and I am dropping with sleep.

MARCH 7TH : MORNING

Still, apparently, no word of the money from
England, except one or possibly two sums to the
Quakers. In the meantime the German Nazis are
sending in money and propaganda—much more
sympathetic and cleverer propaganda than Dollfuss
can do. The Czechs have been fine—they've sent
money, and given much practical help and sympathy. There are constant rumours that there is
Russian money to come, but the Russians will
probably insist on its going through some even
more difficult channel, though their obvious course
(if they've really got it) would be to send it to the
Russian Legation at Prague, and over from there.
Why on earth our money can't be sent to Czecho-
Slovakia, and then over, I don't know. I hear a good
deal of criticism of Deutsch ; he seems to be perfectly
honest, but stupid, rather slow—in many ways a
typical commander of soldiers. He won't see what the
present situation is, or the possibility of keeping the
party alive. But in the meantime —— is still in
Vienna ; they ought to have heard of him at Transport House—not that I had till a few days ago.
Sometimes I think the help has been delayed too
long, and there will certainly be a Nazi—German
Nazi—State here within a few months. At other
times I feel these people are so fine and enduring
that they will be able to stick to Socialism. Again,

133

France seems to be lining up beside Italy—to support the Heimwehr ? ? ?

At mid-morning I went over to Ian's, where there was much discussion. There is still the difficulty of finding somewhere for the man who was in difficulties last night. We find it hard to know quite how seriously to take the police and the spy system ; it is probably very efficient, but equally it will have limitations—the difficulty is to know what. Yesterday, in response to a good deal of Press agitation, a commission went to visit the prisons, from the Press Association here. It was perhaps a pity that the English representative should have happened to be the correspondent of one of our most Fascist dailies. Various people turned up, with news or rumours, including the usual friendly Americans, who seem always to be found. I should like to go to one of the provincial towns, but the others say I ought to stay here. Letters from home had more cheerful news about the money question ; at least the *Genossen* there are getting together. Dick sends magnificently cryptic letters, which provide all the excitement of a cross-word puzzle ! The Quakers have definitely got some money, but seem to be being very cautious about spending it—as though they really were a Government department. There is a good deal of trouble here over the idiotic message in the *Daily Herald*, explaining that 2,500 families are being given thirty Schillings a week—nearly twice the official unemployment insurance pay ! I don't wonder

they are angry. M. is going to Gratz for a few
days.

Janet and I went off to Floridsdorf, by the route I
am beginning to know, passing the bridges and the
piece of old waste land which has been so cleverly and
simply made into a park. From the tram we walked,
again passing these admirable Gemeinde Hauser ;
I had no idea how many there were—how they had
changed the face of the city. One knew of the three
or four buildings which were architecturally most
exciting, but not about these whole districts transformed. In one of these buildings we went up a
staircase, and, after the usual moment of hesitation
and recognition and then the *Freundschaft—Freundschaft* between us, we sat down in the living-room
of a sunny, four-roomed flat. They were big rooms—
this was 13 by 15, I should think, with a wide
window and a door out on to a balcony full of little
pot-plants. At the other side of the table sat a small,
blue-eyed woman, with dark hair streaked with
grey, and face blotched and drawn with anxiety.
She told us her story, or rather the story of her husband and her fourteen-year-old son.

The husband was about forty-six, a gas-worker, a
big, hefty, fair chap, with a strong, unintellectual face,
in a football team. There were four children, of
whom the fourteen-year-old boy was the middle one ;
she showed us his photograph too—a very nice,
friendly face, brown hair, turned-up nose, cocked-up
eyebrows ; rather small, perhaps, but then, he was

born in the bad times. The father was a Schutzbund
leader, and also a well-known local speaker—there
are plenty of men very like him in the King's Norton
Labour Party. He had kept his practical secret
Schutzbund work to himself, not telling his wife, so
as not to implicate her. It is possible that the small
boy may have known more than his mother. On the
Monday of the fighting, Mrs. —— went to the central
wash-house of her building, to do her washing as
usual, not knowing that anything was going to
happen. When she had finished it, she looked out,
and there was the Schutzbund drawn up in the
courtyard. It was her husband who had distributed
arms to them, but she did not know that then. All
Monday evening, and part of Tuesday, there was
fighting. Her husband had three groups to attend to,
all of whom were fighting in different places. Early
on, he lost touch with any central direction, and had
to take the whole responsibility himself. He spent
his time going from one group to another across
Floridsdorf, acting on his own, and nearly distracted
with the strain of it and the lack of communication
with the others.

After the fighting, he was arrested—on the
Thursday. She has not seen him since, although she
has asked to ; some women have seen their men, but
she has not. Why ? The most probable reason seems
to be that he has been so badly beaten up that they
don't want her to see him till most of the marks are
gone. She will not quite admit herself that this is so,

but rumours come from the neighbours. There is a woman in a flat below hers whose man was sentenced to three years' imprisonment ; this woman was at the court when the case was being tried, and brought news that a policeman had told her that her man's former leader has had his nose smashed in.

During the fighting the cinema in the next building, where some Schutzbundlers had been, was fired at, and partly destroyed. It was then shut. On Thursday of the week after the fighting, some boys climbed in, and, seeing it all wrecked, had taken various things which they found lying about. Among them was her boy, who had taken an electric-lamp, and brought it home in triumph. His mother was very much upset ; she had already been visited by the police—on the Sunday—and questioned about her husband. She had said she knew nothing—and, indeed, she knew very little herself. But it had been nerve racking. She took the boy straight off to the caretaker of the staircase where the cinema was, and made him give back the lamp. But the caretaker himself was already terrified ; the police had already heard, and been round and told him that the responsibility for the theft rested with him—and everyone is very much afraid of the police these days. This man had good reason to be, for he had been arrested himself over the fighting, and was only just out of prison again. He said they must themselves go to the police and give up the lamp.

So the mother and son went off together to the police-station, and no doubt the mother scolded the son thoroughly all the way. They saw the head inspector, who was very decent and friendly to them, said that it was a great help that the boy had come himself, but the charge had already gone to the central police-station of Floridsdorf, so the boy must go there. This is the place about which so many terrible stories of beatings are told. The mother told the inspector that she would make the boy find the rest of his gang and make them all give back the things they'd pinched. So they went back, and the boy found two of the others. The three of them went back to the police-station, and from there the inspector sent the boys and their things over to the central commissariat, under police guard.

Here the boy was asked his name, and, when he gave it, and they recognised it, they said, " Your father works in the gas-works ? " " Yes," he said. " Your father has been arrested ? " " Yes." And then two *kriminalbeamter* (plain-clothes men) came along to deal with the boy. " Didn't you know your father gave out weapons ? " " No." " So you don't know anything about your father, either ! You Red rubbish ! Yet, somehow or another, we have four hundred dead." And then they caught the boy by the hair, slung him across the room and down, and, when he was on the floor, kicked him, and hit him across the head and ribs. Probably they didn't particularly want to get information out of him, though no doubt they would have liked any extra evidence against his father, but they just did want to smash up any Red rubbish they could get hold of.

The other boys were knocked about a bit too, but not so much. They were all kept under arrest till 10.15 that evening. There was one policeman, though, who said to the boy, patting his sore shoulder, " Don't worry. Your father is a fine chap." And the boy and his mother both think that this means that the father, under his questioning—and one begins to know what the questioning of a Schutzbundler probably implies—never gave any names.

The mother of one of the other boys came along that evening, and begged the police to let her take back this boy too. They must have meant to keep him, for they had put him into a cell, with two blankets, which they never do for people who are only in for the day, but at last they let her take him away too. He came back, all bruised and cut, his head full of loose hair that had been torn out. He is back at school now. But—— Nobody quite knows what the police mayn't decide to do next.

In the meantime his mother has no money, but the neighbours are very kind ; they give her potatoes and rice. We left a little, from the comrades in *Ausland*. She has been told she must leave her flat. All the Schutzbund people are being turned out, and " safe " families put in instead. She hears that her flat is to be taken over by the police. Other

Schutzbund men have got three years. Her husband was a leader, and well known. He will probably get fifteen or twenty. She doesn't much care what happens. If the prisoners are let free, it's all one to her who frees them. She says that the Nazis and Communists are going to come together and help them. So much for good Nazi propaganda. She waits day after day, "expecting something to happen." So far nothing has. There must be a lot of women waiting.

Janet went back, and I went on to Gartenstadt, where my friend lives, but she was not at home. I think there must have been the maximum of variety among the flats here. In one corner is the great tower, holding up a grand, modern clock-face, which had stopped at 9.30, presumably of Tuesday morning three weeks ago. Under it were the ragged gaps of shell-holes, corners of the tower gnawed off. I went in past two great earthenware flower-pots—or rather one, for the other had been smashed—and up the staircase, no one stopping me. It must have been rather a special staircase, for there was a lift—now not working—and the doors were painted green and panelled ; I think most of the dwellers were professional classes—doctors, for instance. The flats must have been lovely, with balconies and a superb view—now half of them were wrecked.

This building was made between 1926 and 1927—the inner pergolas are perhaps of the taste of seven years ago, not completely modern. Near it are other buildings, not touched. But I went past them, and to visit the family where Evert and I went last week, from which the son had just fled. He is now safe in Brünn, but a few days ago the old parents were visited by the police, who wanted to know where the boy was. When they wouldn't tell, the answer was that, if they could not get at the man they wanted, his family should suffer. I knocked at the door ; the old lady looked out, all of a twitter, but recognised me and let me in ; she had certainly not been shaking like this when I saw her before. Unfortunately I simply couldn't understand the Viennese dialect she spoke. All I got was her constant repetition that the police had come, but she had said nix ; nix (nothing ; nothing). I think, though, that she quite liked seeing me ; I managed to convey good wishes and sympathy if nothing else.

So I came back, and there were lovely cart-horses crossing the bridge, all with bright brass trappings, long strings of leather and brass like golden tresses. It was very late, and I had *Liptauer garniert* and coffee, and then went over to Sam's, after writing some more diary, for them to look over for stories for the Press. One person or another keeps on bringing stories. There is a grim one of the relief work at St. Polten, how it was done inefficiently, so that some of the worst cases among the comrades got nothing. One of these women, a party official, for whom nothing had come, just went mad, went to the police-station, and gave the names of twenty-five party comrades, all of whom were caught by the police.

I like Lass's point of view ; it is so English. She still thinks, in some back part of her mind, that she is being purely non-political. But I know I am working as a Socialist, and I know it is valid. The sense of worth-while-ness, of a centre, of an answer to that Scot-troubling question—What is the Whole End of Man ?—is with me constantly. The *timor mortis*, which I find so bothering at ordinary times, has gone. It is not just that I am too excited, or have too little time, to think of it ; I can think of it calmly, and it has lost its sting. That may come of living with people who value their lives so lightly and gaily ; it's odd to think of the church in the Freiheits-Platz which was vowed by an emperor who escaped assassi-nation—to think of taking oneself so seriously ! But I think that this peculiar validity is the pragmatic sanction of the Marxian theory of *praxis*. It has been, also, the kind of *praxis* which I can understand, the *praxis* of personal relations with other people.

On my way back, I stopped at a post-card shop ; I chose, and bought, some photographs of the Gemeinde Hauser, old and new. As I was about to pay for them, the woman in the shop—an oldish woman—made some remark about them, to which I answered. She said she lived in one, in the tenth district. I answered, I suppose, sympathetically, because she suddenly began to talk, saying how now people say it is wrong to be Red, but Red Vienna

was so beautiful to live in ! And now they had shelled
the houses (again this shocked feeling at the shelling).
Her sister-in-law lived in the Engel Hof (that is the
one just before the bridge over Floridsdorf). They
had arms there, and a Schutzbund company, but
they would not fire on the soldiers who were going
past, because no one had fired on them. She had
heard there was money coming from *Ausland*—was
that true ? Yes, I said, that was true. Someone else
came in, so I said good-bye, and we looked straight
at one another.

More diary, and then Evert and Lisbe, who looks
as though she could deal with him—but mightn't
perhaps want to. Capital yellow hair. Then a girl
turned up to interpret between me and my *Fürsorgerin,* who was actually more than half an hour late,
so that we got rather worried. After a long tram
journey we came at last across a bridge to the Goethe
Hof. It was a dark night and raining a little, but we
could see the black gaps of shell-holes very plainly,
and the heaps of fallen plaster and bricks. We went
in, and up a stair ; a woman greeted us—indoors
another—*Freundschaft.* It was a good flat ; we sat in
the bedroom (there were her own and a neighbour's
children in the living-room), with parquet floor, a
big window and door leading out to the balcony,
twin beds and wardrobes, pot-plants by the window,
a good wallpaper and curtains, and the corners
rounded or slanted for easier cleaning. There were
several of us, and several of them ; the second

woman's husband was at Brünn—she had just heard.
A man came in, one of these small, dark, quick-
moving Viennese, rather like Mr. Priest at King's
Norton ; we all clustered round while he talked.

He began about the fighting, and the women now
and then corroborated. They still always want to
hear the " war-stories "—it's still news to them,
though it may have ceased to be in England. In
this house the Schutzbund had got their arms by
10.30 on the Monday, but had been told not to use
them, nor did they till the other side had begun
firing and had been warned : " If you go on shooting, we fire at you." The Heimwehr had a machine
gun on the tower of the Jubiläum's-Kirche opposite,
on the far side of the river—apparently they had
one there too, on chance, this last First of May.
During the fighting, aeroplanes came over and
signalled to the Government troops. But again I got
the impression that what they really minded was
the shelling—that wasn't part of the game. They
just couldn't get over it.

The man had been taken prisoner on the Tuesday,
and had been in prison for six days. He had been
beaten going down the stairs, and beaten in the
police-court. He had been beaten on the head with
rifle butts. It was the same for others. A man who
had given his room for the wounded Schutzbundlers
had been beaten in the street. One man was now in
hospital with blood-poisoning from a beating. He
gave details. I don't see how these beatings will ever

get out of people's minds, especially the women's. They will have established themselves there as a permanent national or class complex.

Other stories : The seven Heimwehr who went into a woman's flat and stole all her *Schmuck*—her jewellery—smashed up everything, stuck bayonets through the pictures, found two Socialist newspapers, and left them in the flat, having used them as toilet-paper, with a message that she must learn to read religious books. The Heimwehr men who stole spirits and got mad drunk in a café. A few had been arrested, and were in the same police cell as this man. Prisoners were brought into a factory—after the police-station was full—and had to stand all the time with bayonets pointed at them from each side, with no chance of going to a w.c.

Another story : The Radio is now saying that the Socialist leaders have stolen the money and run away with it. But these people don't believe that.

And always the stories of beatings. The prisoners are still only allowed to speak with their friends for a minute or so at a time—if that. At the beginning, when people wanted to take food to their friends, they were not allowed to, only linen and large sums of money—fifty Schillings or over, something impossible for a worker's family. The story of the Schutzbund putting children in the window and firing between their legs has been told about the Goethe Hof mainly. The women explained that they had *not* been warned to take the children away before the shelling (this is the official story), but as soon as it started they all went down into the cellars.

Another story of Schutzbundlers, disguised as soldiers, who ran across the fighting and took two machine guns—but had to give them up in the end. The soldiers themselves became untrustworthy, and had to be changed for other regiments. The police were utterly exhausted. The story of the Schutz-bundlers who loaded a lorry with machine guns and rifles, and drove it all out for the frontier—and got across, because no one stopped them. But twelve from here have been shot on the frontier. And more than two hundred have been arrested.

MARCH 8TH

I found what I saw this morning extremely moving, and so, before writing anything I have read several chapters of Southey's *The Doctor*, which I had brought with me, and darned my stockings—so that I should not write with my body still flooded with anger. Now I must first go on with yesterday.

I asked whether many workers were going Nazi. The man said not many. He added that the Nazis had wanted to help with the revolution, but they

would not let them—they would not let it be said
by the Nazis that they had won anything for the
workers ! But the Communists did come in, and
fought side by side with the Social Democratic
workers. I got the impression that Social Democratic
feeling was very strong ; they were only waiting for
some kind of organisation—however dangerous,
however secret—and then they would work at it
as they had never worked before. I even got the
feeling that here at least the best men had not gone
over the frontier but were still at home, and respected
for it. Yet I don't see how Schutzbund men who are
actually wanted and known by the police can
possibly stay. I feel that there might be a tremendously strong party here in a few years. Even the
Christians, they said, don't hold with what has been
done to us !

More stories of beatings—a sixty-three-year-old
man taken and beaten. They are only waiting for a
chance to hit back, now. Starhemberg came to the
Goethe Hof (this was where Evert counted, himself,
forty-two bodies laid out in the wash-house), and
said, " Far too few shot." That will be remembered ;
no amount of clemency propaganda will obliterate it.

More about the searches for arms. But the police
who came later were decent, just opened the cup-
boards, looked in, and went away. I asked if I could
see a house that had been searched. The woman who
had done most of the talking said yes, she thought so.
None of my friends could come, and seemed a little

doubtful about my going by myself, but I said, firmly, I was all right, and the woman agreed that it was much better for a single person to come. She and I had summed one another up. I agreed to be there at 11.30 the next morning.

I asked about Soziale-Hilfe. One woman said that the ladies had been, and given her a food-packet, the day before yesterday (for the first time). There was a pound of rice, a pound of meal, a pound of coffee, ground rice, oranges, and so on. There was nothing in the nature of propaganda, and they had been quite nice. On leaving, they had said : " *Auf Wieder-sehen.* And you mustn't look so cross at us next time." She had got no money from them, but a little through the Friends, which she definitely took to be party money—it must, indeed, almost certainly have been part of the lump sum which was sent out from England, but which must be now finished.

What I want to make clear now is the fierce anti-clericalism that burns in these people—it flamed out from the little group of workers, and met an answering fierceness from the *Fürsorgerin.* It isn't to be wondered at when one considers how little the Church counts, except as a political instrument. That is certainly how they regard it—for the satisfying of the religious sense they must go elsewhere—to the comrades, to *Freundschaft* and *Freiheit.* The first school-day after the fighting, the children were told they must go to a thanksgiving service. Here they were preached at, told that " Red dogs wanted to make a bloody field of revolution in Vienna, but Dollfuss and Fey have prevented this." The thirteen-year-old-son of the woman who was speaking—I will call her Frau M.—refuses to go any more. But his mother is rather worried about that ; to get on at school nowadays one must get good marks in religion !

The *Konfessionslosen* are being forced, by economic circumstances, back into the Catholic Church ; those who can, join the Protestants or Old-Catholics, anything rather than the hated Roman Church, which supports the Austrian Fascist Party, the Heimwehr. Adults are being baptised every day ; it is extremely awkward for the really religious priests, who cannot truthfully believe in a change of heart among these new applicants for admission, but who yet cannot decently refuse them what is in fact the only way now to get a job. There are adult " preparation classes " going on, where no doubt the priest has rather an uncomfortable time, too. Frau M. told us of one class. A woman asked, " What is God ? " " God is a free spirit." " But then He can be followed anywhere." " No, no ; only in the Catholic Church." One woman complains, " Here are Austrian Christians and Italian Christians and French Christians and German Christians, all taking up arms, all wanting to fight one another. And yet you say Christianity is brotherhood. How ? Does one shoot one's brothers ? " Another woman : " That is the Catholic International ! " The priest : " Children,

children, please, no politics here ! " I heard a story from Janet, of a catechist, taking a class of the older girls from a school, looking round and glaring at them as he came in, and saying : " It's as well we've come into power, otherwise you'd be on the streets ! "

Frau M. was pouring out stories now—she was good at them : The woman in the smashed flat who said to the Heimwehr man : " You can take everything from me, everything, but here within I have a place in my heart, *ein Roter Fleck* (a Red splash)." The woman who let foreigners come and photograph her wrecked flat—when they wanted to arrest her for doing so, and said she ought to be ashamed of herself, she said to them : " I am not ashamed to let them see ; it is my pride ! It is you who ought to be ashamed ; you who destroyed it." Stories like this go round from mouth to mouth, part of a new heroic legend, the women taking on after the men are dead or arrested.

So many people come to see the Goethe Hof that the doors are closed in the afternoon. The people from the smashed flats are distributed among neighbours. X gave the woman twenty Schillings for distribution " from the comrades "—she tucked it down her neck into her bodice. " Everything goes there," she said, laughing. " Names, addresses, literature, everything ! " A capital woman.

Coming back, they told me about the new Reichsbrücke—construction on it had started—it was to be a big job, but all workers had not only to belong to the Vaterländische Front, but to be " Christliche Gerwerkschafter " (member of the " Christian " Trades Union) as well ! *Um Gotteswillen*, as they say what would the founder of this religion—of this political party—have said to that ? He'd be kicking the money-changers out of the Temple all right !

I got back to the hotel about 9.30, very hungry, and hoping, also, for a bath, as I haven't had one for days. *Dis aliter visum*. I found a wire, saying I was to write an article for *Reynolds's*—that meant getting it off by air-mail that night. There was also rather a cheering and hopeful letter from Dick. I now realise that why he wasn't in when I telephoned was that the time is different here—I actually rang him up at the wrong time. It's the sort of idiotic thing one forgets.

I spent the evening, then, writing diary and the article. I pitched things hot and strong into the latter, but I don't think I was ever untruthful. But one has to break down such a stone wall of ignorance and prejudice, and, above all, not-caring, that one has to hit hard. I'm awfully glad they're taking it.

This morning Janet rang up early, to ask if I could come round. I went, picking up, on my way, a letter which enclosed cuttings from *The Times*, mostly about Amery's speech to the Unionist Association in Birmingham, all about how the Austrian revolution was made by a few extremists—beautiful dream of the Conservative Party always !—how the municipal tenement houses which had been made into fortresses were disarmed, and how Dollfuss, the " great little man " was going to win over everyone by his clemency ! One always hopes that the other side do this kind of thing accidentally, through having a different vision, as it were. But I felt ashamed then that Amery should have read my books. Probably he never will again, that's something !

Janet was very much upset about Frau B., the wife of one of the men who were hanged in the first day's anger, and now a hero whose name everyone knows. She has already been worried by the police, asked to change her name—there was an attempt, I believe, to take away her two small children—and now it is essential, for her health, that she should leave Austria. Friends in England have asked her to stay, but she hasn't a pass ; there are already signs that she may not get one. Janet suggested that I could go to the Legation, but I thought it would be better to go with rather more to show—a direct refusal, for instance.

Then came a longish wait—the usual thing—while we discussed various things, fidgeting, wondering what was going to happen, angry with the newspapers for having so much news and so little that we wanted to read. Then a phone call from Sam, asking me to go straight to see S. Having no small change, I borrowed two Schillings from Mary—our money is very communal !—and took a taxi across. There I found nice, friendly S., less nervous than when I saw him last—presumably he has been seeing less of the police—and the Geneva correspondent, with whom I, and, later, Sam, discussed things. So odd, this newspaper world—writers, and yet how unlike highbrow writers ! Applied writing. But can writing be ever " pure," like " pure " science ? Perhaps some of the experimenters. Gertrude Stein, Joyce—and at the moment I simply can't feel they matter two pins. S. said I looked Viennese, which I took as a compliment, though rather a fantastic one, considering my very English tweeds, my solid laced shoes (from Dowie and Marshall), and my woollen stockings and cap (from Oban) ! However, I don't make up, any more than most people here seem to do—as opposed to France or England.

I caught a tram—I'm beginning to find my way about. There was a capital man sitting in it, with a Tyrolese hat, and a waxed and curled moustache. I changed trams, and got off and began to walk towards the Goethe Hof ; a woman asked me if I lived there (which confirms S.'s theory !), and began to talk about it. As I came near in the daylight—it was very dark last night—I realised that it had been worse hit than any of the houses I have yet seen, except the Arbeiterheim in Ottakring. Frau M. came to meet me, and shook hands with the woman I'd been talking to, then tucked an arm under mine, and walked in with me. I should probably have been all right going in by myself, but there are a good many police and Heimwehr about.

The inner courtyard is magnificent, and profits by having one fine tree—most of the others have only the young trees which were planted when the places were built. There is a school and playground, of which they are obviously proud. And, by the way, the *Kinderfreunde* here (a Socialist organisation for children, which has, of course, like all the clubs, been closed) had a chest full of tools for children, worth about 200 Schillings, stolen by the Heimwehr. There are children playing in the courtyard, but one whole corner is horribly smashed, and there are bullet-marks everywhere. I simply don't see how it can ever be properly repaired, short of a thorough rebuilding of one part. As Frau M. looked, she squeezed my arm convulsively—she wasn't used to it yet !

We went up the corner stair. At the bottom had been the café ; there had been a direct hit, and then a fire ; the place was more or less gutted ; it looked so stupid, so unnecessary, these tables and chairs upset, the plush seats broken and scorched, all the rather ugly but quite pleasant accompaniments of people living together, drinking and smoking, and playing games and reading newspapers—and now it was all finished ! The women and children from that stair had been immediately below, on the landing, when the café was struck ; they must have been deafened, and covered with plaster and brick-dust.

154

We climbed the stair, passing one or two others. No one spoke, except in a whisper. We came to an upper flat. It had been completely smashed ; floor and walls alike broken into dust and ragged holes. I couldn't see how it could possibly be put right. An electric-light shade dangled beads, almost whole ; otherwise there was no recognisable piece of furniture, except the crumpled gas-stove and part of a bed—as I stooped over it, feathers flew up in my face from what had once been a mattress. Frau M. stood in the dust and rubble, fiercely thinking of Them—Them !—who had done this, who had shot the Goethe Hof from the Jubiläum's-Kirche across the river. The woman whose flat it had been came in, aimlessly ; she and her child are living with neighbours. She came up to me, we took hands, and whispered, "*Freundschaft*," and then she looked again—for the hundredth, for the thousandth time perhaps—at the holes and rubbish, and her face began to twitch. Frau M. went over to her, and took her by the shoulders, speaking quickly, earnestly ; the other woman shook her head. "I can't speak," she said. "Ich bin stumm." Her hand flickered to her face and back ; she looked round again, and there was nothing. Frau M. got hold of me now, saying, "She has nothing ; nothing but the clothes she stands up in !" There were tears in her eyes too ; she picked up a bit of something from the rubbish, dropped it again. They looked from one to the other. It was unbearable. I thought that in a minute I

155

would be crying too. I said : " I will tell this to the
workers of England." And Frau M. turned to me
with her hands clasped. " Do that ! " she said.
" Do it ! " And I promised I would, and I wrote
in my note-book for a moment, till suddenly there
was a whisper : " Somebody coming ! " And I
jammed my note-book into my pocket, completely
caught in this atmosphere of terror and secrecy.
But it was only the woman's child, small and white-
faced, come to look too—poking at the remains of his
engine and his aeroplane, bothered by it all, supposing, perhaps, that ordinary life was going to
begin again some day.

The woman picked up the remains of a man's
shirt, and dropped it. She reached a hand to the
wall, and patted it ; dust fell away as she did so.
" Aber es ist meine Wohnung," she said. " But it's
my little house." I put my arm round her shoulder.
I said, " I will tell ; it will not be forgotten." But
now she was crying again, quietly.

I asked if she had got anything from the Soziale-
Hilfe. " No," she said. " Nix—nothing." The
Regierung doesn't care. We went to another flat,
equally destroyed, the only thing a bad oil-painting
on the wall, with just two or three holes in it. Above
it was worse, everything incredibly twisted and
jagged and broken, and, through the window,
broken roofs and holes in walls and splinters of glass
in the window-frames. There was a coating of plaster
over everything, plaster dust still in the air. They tell

me that the women and children here were *not* warned before the shelling, as was reported. Perhaps some of them were.

In another flat—here, too, the woman was crying ; her husband had died three weeks before the fighting —a shell had wrecked one room and partly wrecked the other ; there were the typical claw-marks of shell splinters in the floor and the door of the wardrobe. After that, the Heimwehr had come and looted ; they had taken all the husband's old clothes which she still had.

The second court is as fine as the first, but I don't think the people who live in it can see it as beautiful any longer. They only see it marred by the shell-holes. What the shelling leaves behind is extraordinarily ugly—things that ought to be straight, bent up and crippled—things men have made, broken up, and their insides showing, and an ugliness which makes one think of the ugly noise there must have been, the screaming of wood and metal torn apart. I expect that's hard to forget too.

We went out of the central court ; above the gateways are three good statues ; somehow or another they've escaped, though there are bullet-marks all round them. That's good, but the people are still too unhappy and shocked to think of it. And now we took a tram, some way, back across the bridge and out into another of the workers' districts. And so we came to a four-roomed wooden house, with a little garden, hen-house, rabbit hutches, and a vine. In front is a trellis, with a door in it ; the woman of the house let us through. Here the lands between the city and the rising hills, with their pine-woods, are dotted with allotments and hen-runs, and funny little wooden houses, peasant houses, each with a smoking chimney and a watch-dog, and a porch with creepers over it. This particular little house was one of the first half dozen to be built here— right outside the city of those days.

Outside the house, on a railing, was hung a pink, feather bed-quilt. It had already been washed twice, but it still had the marks of urine on it. Also outside, on a bench, were fifteen or twenty jars of marmalade and jam, each of which had had a bayonet jabbed through the cover. Inside in the first room, there was " HUNDE—HUNDE " scratched deep into the walls. The mirror was a little cracked, but mostly the Heimwehr had contented themselves with throwing eggs at it. We went into the next room, and here the old lady brought out of the cupboard—which itself had been prised open with bayonets—a violin or what had been a violin. But the case had been smashed open and the violin, I should say, stamped upon. So much for *Gemütlichkeit*.

I sat at the table while the old lady talked, in a thick Viennese accent, which my friend translated into German. She had lived hereabouts all her life, and so had her man. When they were married, he had built this house himself. " Es war unser Heilig-tum," she said. The children had been born here.

158

Her man was a machine worker, and must have done well ; he had been a member of the Social Democratic Party since 1885—a William Morris-Hyndman Socialist, as it were. She too, she said proudly, was a party member. He was sixty-four, and she had been sixty on the Wednesday immediately after the fighting. Her children had sent her cakes and schnapps. There was a wooden tray quite full of cakes ! Her house had not been hurt by the cannon-fire in the quarters near by ; and on the Thursday, the day after her birthday, she went to have dinner with her daughter. Obviously she never thought anything would happen to *her* ; everyone knew her, people of all parties ; everyone liked her, and came to her when they were in trouble. She was a kindly, tough old lady—never ill a day all her life. She was the grandmother of the district ; had watched the new Gemeinde Hauser go up ; was friends with everyone. And then——

She came back from dinner with her daughter, and found the Heimwehr had been in her home, searching for weapons. I asked if they'd had any. But she said no, she and her husband were too old for that. And I said, " I hope at least there are some arms which are still hidden ! " " Hoffentlich ! " said Frau M., and the old woman nodded—she felt like that too. She came into her house. Everything was quite incredibly messed up, flour and coffee thrown about—they'd walked in that and trampled it about the place. They'd overset the stove and

thrown the coals about. They had killed her cat.
They had prised open everything with bayonets,
thrown out the linen and fouled it themselves.
Everything had to be washed—two or three times.
They had bayoneted up the linoleum. They had
torn up the children's books, and Socialist books,
including some the husband had since 1885. They
had eaten all her birthday-cakes, and drunk ten
litres of schnapps—having drunk it, they'd rolled
about on the bed with the result I'd already
seen.

They had also stolen a good many things, including
a gramophone and twenty-three records ; a camera ;
playing-cards ; a leather case ; stockings ; a watch
and clock ; a silver cigarette-case ; the rent-book,
and other documents ; a gold ring ; a gold chain ;
a golden bracelet, which had belonged to their
foster-child, who died ; a sham pearl necklace ; a
comb—every sort of thing. And they had smashed
the violin, which was worth one hundred and twenty
Schillings. They had stolen a cushion on which
she had embroidered *Freiheit*—she minded that a
lot. They only took three Schillings in money, but
that was because she had taken her purse out with
her.

The only thing they had left behind was a prayer-
book, belonging to one of them ; it had his name in it.
She told me the name. That same evening a young
man from the Heimwehr came back to ask for his
prayer-book, and to give in exchange two gold

rings (one broken) and a wrist-watch ! Still later, the Landesgericht—the higher court—sent back the gramophone and records, the camera, and a few small oddments. I don't suppose she's likely ever to get the rest back.

She took me through to the rest of the house ; there were bayonet-marks everywhere, which couldn't be cleared up, though the dirt—the *Schmutz*—had gone. There was her tiny kitchen, all so neat and German, like a doll's-house kitchen. They were such decent people, a man and woman who'd been honest and hard-working and thinking (it took some thought to be a Social Democrat forty years ago), who had led a good life, loving their neighbours, friendly to everyone. And then these foul little Heimwehr boys had come. I made them a speech. I didn't know I knew that much German. I said it should be remembered and made right, that *Ausland* should be told. I think they were glad of that.

This woman, too, had got nothing from the official help. She said, " We hear there is help coming from England—when ? " And I said yes, it was coming ; it really was, but in the English party, too, there was bureaucracy ; there were difficulties. They laughed and understood. But they would like the money. My God, when is it going to come ?

I took the tram back with my friend. She asked, " What will the English workers say ? " I tried to explain that they were slow, but they would see at

last, and then I began to wonder if they ever *would*
see—if I should ever have understood myself, if I
hadn't had it all under my own eyes. If only I can
make it plain !

She said again, "When comes the help from
England ? " And I had to say I didn't know, but
it was really coming, we had a *Genosse* coming out
this evening—he might know. We were trying to
get it. And they, in turn, they must keep the party
going, so that in time over there by the new bridge-
end there would be the Red flag flying instead of the
Dollfuss flag. And she sighed, and looked at the
hills—the Wiener Wald, crowned with castles and
woods, a most beautiful bluish purple under a soft
sky—and she said, " I lived here three and a half
years. I cannot bear to live here now." And
again, " Es war so schön in Wien, wunderbar schön
war es." You see, I think the point of this is that
these are people who really do care for beauty, for
all the things that story-book Vienna cares for. It
was *they* who had the *Gemütlichkeit*, they in the light,
friendly Gemeinde Hauser, and not the shop-
keepers and civil servants of the centre. It is because
of this, because they had this feeling for beauty—
and that may have been partly inborn, and partly
through living with it in the beautiful houses, for
I know that the way one lives alters one's thought
and standards—that it was a crime against civilisation to shell them. Here were people getting a little
near to the Greeks of the fifth century—beauty with

economy—and we have let them be killed and discouraged and mocked at.

I believe I am right over this. I believe that suffering and ugliness are relative, are a matter of standards. It *does* matter less that animals should be hurt (say) than that children should be hurt. It does matter less that uncivilised, less aware, less conscious people should be killed and hurt than really civilised, æsthetically, and socially aware people. And these Viennese workers, they were valuable to the world, to mankind ; they were gay and brave and friendly; they had the good manners that come of living well in the heart. It does matter to the whole of civilisation that they should have been smashed up. For the sake of mankind and the future, as well as for the sake of Socialism (which is perhaps the same thing), they must be helped and saved, in so far as in us lies. If this helping and saving and encouraging implies going behind the back of any Government, well, that can't be helped. One really can't allow oneself to be bound by the notions of inferior, or less far-sighted persons. What is education for except to teach one when one must act for oneself—when the spirit must stalk free across these idiotic boundaries of Governments and groups ?

MARCH 9TH

It looked like being a peaceable day yesterday.
I spent the afternoon writing diary, and even a letter
or two, waiting for Sam to ring up, as he had said
he would, but didn't till late. Janet came round in
the evening, and we dined together. She had one or
two pretty horrid stories, especially about conditions
at St. Pölten, and also told me about the new
Government decree by which any doctor, lawyer,
or chemist who gets a political police-court sentence,
of even a few hours, loses not only his job, but also
his title by which he professes his job. No doubt this
will particularly apply to some of the young doctors
who have been doing illegal work on humanitarian
grounds.

Then Glyndwr turned up from England—I'd got
rather worried about his not coming earlier, but he
had gone to Sam's, not having realised that I was
here. We had all hoped much from his coming,
having the vain and even hysterical idea that he
might actually arrive with the official money, or at
least some definite news of its arrival. But no such
luck. In England they still seem to think that
everything can be done legally and without haste.
He had various messages though. The N.F.R.B.
have some conception of the situation, and are
trying to centralise propaganda and open a fund for
" difficult " cases. There's some money for me from

them and from Dick, so that at least we've got a margin to go on. Glyndwr unloaded himself of a grand collection of fivers ! I'm not too keen on having a bank account here, in case of having to leave suddenly.

I talked things over with him for some time, and arranged to meet Sam at midnight at a café opposite. Poor Glyndwr rather groaned, for he had come third, and had little sleep, but I was firm. My first *Herald* article had appeared, and there was a letter asking for another, more topical one—not " war stories." They want my name to them ; apparently they don't realise that not only may it be very awkward for me to sign things, but also it may be really dangerous for the people I write about. After a time, I reluctantly decided that I ought to send the article off that night, and had done a third of it by midnight, when we went over to the café.

Glyndwr, being a Celt, is rather good at picking up atmospheres ; he seemed to get it almost at once. He has the curious gloom and unbelief of the modern young man, all on a basis of hereditary chapel mentality ; but I believe Vienna can deal even with that. We waited in the café till one a.m.— slightly cheered by a visit from C.—and talked ; then Sam turned up, and we bought sausages—he'd had no dinner—and bread, chocolate, and oranges, at a stall, and came back to my room to discuss things. Glyndwr promised to write various letters, explaining the situation ; he has one excellent comic-opera

165

accomplishment—he can write in Welsh ! In the meantime, and constantly joining in the conversation at those moments when I felt I had to disagree, I finished my *Herald* article. It was three a.m. when I'd finished it, and the conversation finished itself —I've now no idea what I said in the article. . . . But Sam posted it, and we all agreed to sleep late and not ring one another up till we absolutely had to.

The morning seemed quiet ; Glyndwr and Evert and I are all on this floor, so that we can trot in and out of one another's rooms. I went and had a long walk with ——, tired as usual. We discussed the future of the Austrian Socialist Party, all finally ending in practical agreement. It seems fairly plain that the Dollfuss Government has crushed democracy, though it has not crushed Socialism. So the workers' party must now cease to be democratic— how can it be when it is working illegally ?—and must instead adopt revolutionary tactics. If these succeed it will establish itself, and ultimately win ; then for a time there must be a period of the dictatorship of the proletariat, just till the Fascist forces are disarmed and made economically powerless. Even while this is going on, democracy can be being restated and practised within the Socialist Party, and, when it is complete, democracy of the new kind can become a reality in Austria. None of us are willing to consider an Austria on the Russian plan ; we believe in the same kinds of freedom as seem necessary for the happiness of the average

166

Englishman (and which he calls democracy) ; but we do realise that nice, legal, representational methods are no longer possible, and we must do things in the only practical way. The old heads of the Social Democratic Party, who are in Prague, have given up the leadership, and the new people must take it on whatever way seems best. I am a democrat, but I realise that I cannot live as a democrat in a non-democratic State, any more than I can live as a consistent Socialist in a capitalist State. I also know that England, for instance, is not a democracy—I am a sufficiently good historian for that fact to be plainer to me than it is to some eminent publicists—and that the idea has to be restated, perhaps not now, but in another fifty years. But I hope I shall live to see it done.

We do not any of us take the Communist point of view ; we are, I hope, more constructive than that, and more aware of the real feelings of the workers. We are not, of course, in complete agreement, but quite sufficiently to work together.

Then Glyndwr, Sam, and I went off to lunch at a small restaurant, which, for some obscure reason, one went into, not through the entrance, but from a courtyard behind ; that seemed rather typical ! We had a good meal—though Vienna is purgatory for those who don't like caraway-seeds. So back. I shouted hallo, across the space between our windows, to Evert, who called back excitedly that I was to come round at once ; and, when I did, I found Lisbe, who explained that she and Lass had been arrested that morning in Floridsdorf, and kept for three hours, being interrogated at the police-station. Odd to think I'd been getting a little bored, wanting to leave Vienna for some more interesting place! Glyndwr and Sam came round, beaming with excitement, and we proceeded to ring up everyone. First we got hold of an Anglo-American correspondent, who is always a good friend of ours, and made an appointment; he was very busy, and didn't awfully want to be interrupted, but, when I slipped it across that two English women had been arrested, he became all professional, and I almost saw him rubbing his hands down the telephone! The Legation was less successful—everyone was indefinitely out. But I talked to some bottle-washer, like an Outraged Englishwoman (Evert giggled in a corner), and I finally got an appointment, and put on what I thought were suitable clothes to look Outraged in. My *best* silk stockings. . . .

It appeared that they had been given away by the little schoolmaster from whom both they and I had got lists of names. It immediately occurred to us that —— might also be involved. Yet the more I thought about the little teacher, the less I thought he could have done it maliciously. He was so obviously sincere. He must have been horribly frightened before he did it.

Lisbe wasn't frightened, indeed she was really rather thrilled. I rang up Lass, and told her she'd

got to come along with me and be an Outraged
Englishwoman too. I was glad I hadn't been there—
I very nearly had been—as I should certainly have
got panicked. As it was, I was enjoying it, and so was
Sam, and so was Evert, as it would work nicely in
with his last article to the *Auchtermuchty Advertiser*.
I was really feeling what fun, and then I thought of
the little teacher with his dark frightened eyes, and
all our friends in Floridsdorf who hadn't got nice
blue passports and Legations and Oxford accents,
and could be atrociously bullied and frightened into
doing things they had never meant to do. And I
thought of the people all over the world who can
be bullied and done down like that, and who could
never even answer back, and then it stopped being
such fun, and I felt real anger. And I did most
awfully want that little man not to have been hurt.

Sam and I picked up Lass—her Jake had got
chickenpox, and a very scarlet small face glared at
us angrily when we came in. Her story was that she
had been to various houses with Lisbe, ending up
with a woman to whom she had been before to get
new names. There was a strange man sitting at the
table, who produced his police badge, and told them
they must come with him to the police-station.
There she was examined, but, as Lisbe's German is
pretty bad, she got off better. She was confronted
with the teacher's story, and explained how she had
got the names through Jake's school, and had gone
round on her own, quite unpolitically, to help

distressed families—she doesn't, after all, belong to any political party herself ! Then the teacher himself was brought in, under arrest, and looking very bothered and unhappy. He had some quite fantastic story of how he had met her in a café, but she had already given her true story, and had to stick to it. After that she was questioned again, asked why she had taken money to the guilty—the *Schuldige*—rather than to the *Unschuldige*, of whom she might have got a list from the police. She answered that she was only concerned with children, and was working on purely humanitarian lines. The police tried hard to make her admit she was one of the Quakers—*diese Quäker* !—for they are obviously trying to get some handle against the Quakers. But, again, she did not admit it—nor, indeed, has she ever worked in connection with them. They tried to get her to admit that she had done wrong—still she wouldn't. They wanted her to realise how naughty it was of foreigners to give money to women whose husbands were actually in prison ! No good. She was British !

She tells me that they seemed to know nothing about the Dollfuss–Innitzer fund, which is theoretically trying to help the *Schuldige* as well, though it isn't particularly successful. The police had some soup kitchen of their own, that was all. While being passed about from one policeman to another, she saw various people, whom she knew by sight, under arrest in the corridors. While she was waiting, she heard some of them being examined—loud voices, and thumping on the table, but couldn't hear what was said. The final inspector was more sympathetic, and said, smiling a little, that he supposed she had Socialist leanings. She shrugged her shoulders, and said, " What can you expect ? " They were let out about two o'clock. She had rung up her hostess, but fortunately not the Consulate—or the story might have been spoiled.

Well, that was news for us, especially as it confirmed us in our view that the police hate the Quakers and want a chance of stopping them. It was funny to think how dull the day had looked like being ! We went straight to the café to find our Anglo-American correspondents, who were delighted, some as journalists, and some as sympathisers. " Now," said an American, " my paper will take all the things they've cut out before ! This is front-page news, and I can get across my stories of destitution in Floridsdorf." Then G. proceeded to sketch out some nice headlines. Half-way through, he suspected me—and rightly—of making notes about him. I wanted to get his eager, pleased face, his cocked eyebrows, the air of a child who's at last got the biggest cake ! But we didn't want anyone to make a scoop of it—before we left we had started them off ringing up all their colleagues—they too could use it to get across their real news. That was the point of it, and the reason we felt ourselves able to go on and pretend to make a fearful fuss about it.

We went to the Legation, and waited a few minutes

till suddenly someone realised who we were. I
noticed my former friend disappearing hastily round
a door, while we were ushered into the presence of
the Minister himself, with a check tie, wavy hair, and
a nice, clean, scarcely lined public-school face. He
was really rather bothered with our story, which
Lass told admirably, while I stood by to catch, and
Lisbe looked like a nice young thing. He said he
would take the matter up, and obviously meant to,
but then went on to say that of course conditions
were really almost all right in Vienna. At that Lass
and I jumped down his throat, with present-day
brutalities and terrorism. I think he was really upset.
It must be an exceedingly difficult position for him,
with the Simon policy of non-interference, so that he
really can't do much. Naturally, he believes what he
ought to believe. And there are certain things which
don't come his way. No one has cried on his shoulder
in Floridsdorf. That sort of thing makes a difference.
I was really very sorry for him, but, of course, if
one's a diplomat, then a diplomat one has to be.

He asked me my view of the political situation,
which flattered me, as no doubt it was meant to do.
But still, it is always nice to be taken seriously ! I
gave him a selection of my views, as calmly and
reasonably as possible, hoping they would impress
him. I don't think he realises that Dollfuss is as
fiercely hated as he is—he still thinks that Dollfuss
might be the head of a popular Government,
whereas I know that's impossible. I told him various

things I'd seen, and he said how nice it would be if journalists were to bring him their facts as soon as they got them. I agreed that it would be nice, and warned him that most of the journalists I knew had got a lot of facts just lately, and were likely to pour them out on the world. He seemed worried. Of course, they have the actual power, while he has the shadow—and obligations—of it. But at the same time I didn't feel that he and I were really in the same world.

We came back to our Press conference, and found the table surrounded by journalists, who fell on us as eagerly as dogs on a bone. It was really rather impressive, though extremely difficult not to laugh, they looked so funny. They were mostly male, but such different shapes ! Fat journalists and angular journalists and streamlined journalists—the *Manchester Guardian*, thick and intelligent ; the *Herald*, small and friendly and accurate ; the *Express*, with sleeked black hair, asking questions hard—women and children first ; the *New York Times*, superbly fat ; Evert, too young a journalist to have quite the eyebrows or the shamelessness. Lass told her story excellently and truthfully—admitted to her aristocratic relationship with rather a groan, but still it was all in a good cause. Their eyes opened, and they scribbled hard. When everyone else had gone,—— of the —— —— turned up, and he was the funniest of the lot. I couldn't quite believe he was real. Occasionally G. winked at me—*he* saw !

So back to dinner and writing this (though again I was so tired I broke off in the middle, and am now writing the next day . . .).

MARCH 10TH

I am so tired I shan't be able to finish writing to-day, and to-morrow we start at 7.15. When I get back I shall sleep and sleep and sleep.

A tiring and rather fruitless morning—I had hoped to go to St. Pölten with G., but it didn't come off. We had hoped to borrow a car, or else hire one, but it got later and later ; people said they would get us names or ring someone up—said, "Just a minute," and disappeared for hours ! It might have been Moscow. . . . The usual crowd, everyone pleased with the newspapers, which are beginning to wake up—it looks almost as though Austria were news again in England—we felt ourselves justified of our labours. Perhaps Transport House even will wake up.

M. back from Graz and Leoben, where she had seen a prison—fearfully overcrowded, but otherwise all right. A splendid local lawyer was doing his best to organise the defence of the prisoners. By the way, the lawyer who was going to defend Frau

Wallisch, and to whom I had paid some money of my own, has been arrested.

We read the papers, and talked to one another—spread rumours—wondered what was going to happen—when the money would come—whether the Quakers would get into a row—what had happened at the L.C.C. elections, even. None of us could go out (I terribly want to get my hair washed, and I must make various small purchases), because we were all waiting for telephone messages—or for someone else. Janet had the usual crop of horrors. Ian was fearfully worried over one thing and another. We could all have done with an extra hour's sleep. G. was cheerful when he came along, preceded, as usual, by Strupye, whom we have decided is an Arian dog, blond and affectionate and violent, and without much intellect. But I can't imagine G. *not* cheerful.

At lunch Sam and ——, also a little worried. There are one or two unpleasant possibilities about. Whenever I get qualms of conscience, they are sweet to me, and say, " Poor Naomi ! " It is, I suppose, really rather nice and international that my Scotch conscience should be the laughing-stock of Social Democratic Vienna ! And what dears they are.

Glyndwr and I started off after lunch—I had promised G. to take him down to see some of my Floridsdorf friends. According to him, this was quite safe, as the police were now very apologetic—say it's all a case of mistaken identity (which it obviously isn't), and that anyway they were only kept for half an hour (which is a plain lie). But at least they are exceedingly unlikely to have anything on me, or to interfere with any more foreigners in Floridsdorf for a day or two.

Half-way to G.'s we passed two large and orderly processions of men in ordinary clothes, marching, in military fashion, towards the Rathaus. We asked three bystanders who they were. The first answered that he didn't know, and hastily moved on ; the second grinned, and said they were out for a *Spaziergang*, and the third made a slight face, and said they were harmless. We discovered later that they were civil servants going to make a spontaneous demonstration—to assist which, loud-speakers had spontaneously sprung up by the Rathaus. While, earlier that day, each had found a leaflet spontaneously lying on his desk to tell him all about it.

I was still feeling rather sick about the Lass and Lisbe " story," as, I am quite certain, they were. Certainly neither of them would have made a fuss about it if they hadn't been driven to by the necessities of the situation. It seemed so idiotic that, when two people with big blue passports were kept in a police-station for three hours, hundreds of others, without blue passports, could be bullied and beaten for days at that same police-station without its ever becoming news ! But our friends had managed, because of them, to get all kinds of things into their papers which they would otherwise have had

to leave unsaid. We all went down to Floridsdorf,
and the lovely Gartenstadt. G. had been there last
in the middle of the fighting, and was interested to
see the effect of the shells that he'd watched being
fired.

My friend, Mrs. T., wasn't in, but I knocked at
the door of the neighbours, whom I knew to be
O.K. They were pleased to see us, and, after
Freundschafts all round, we all went and sat in the
kitchen, while a tame bird fluttered about, and a
dog came and made friends with G., as dogs always
do. We talked of conditions, and they asked if I'd
got the photo of Deutsch which had been sent me
(as also a slip, printed in red, warning Socialists
against the *Kleine Blatt*—so many don't realise it
has been taken over by the Government). I said I
had, and then G. produced a better copy of the
photograph (which has been reproduced cheaply,
and is circulating everywhere), and told them he had
got the photo for publication direct from Deutsch
himself! They were immensely pleased, and then
asked if it was true that Deutsch had been blinded,
and had one arm shot off—G., of course, said, " No "
(and did the same when Mrs. T. asked the same
question). There is a great Deutsch legend going
about ; he comes in for plenty of criticism from the
party intelligentsia—and rightly—but the rank and
file have made him a hero—and perhaps rightly
too, for he has all the simple heroic qualities.

In this household the mother—or aunt, I'm not

sure which—is still in prison. She is accused of
having taken ammunition out to the men ; actually
she took tea and coffee. Her youngest son is in prison
too, and one of the others has been subpœnaed to act
as evidence against his mother. Her trial comes off
on the 23rd, and she has had no legal help.

When Mrs. T came back, we went over to her
house. I told her what had happened to Lass. She
was upset, but not really surprised, she has acquaintances among the police, who warned her that something was up, and she had been wondering how to
warn Lass not to come on Tuesday. Now she says
she will come to her that morning instead, and hopes
to bring some addresses in Ottakring where no help
has yet been given. She tells me that there is gossip
about, and that the husband of a girl cousin of hers,
who is helping us too over this business of collecting
difficult cases and getting money to them (he is
some kind of minor official in a municipal office)
has been warned that his pay will be cut if they find
out that she has been helping to distribute the
foreign money—but her cousin had asked for more
money, and she took 180 Schillings from me, for
the cousin to give to people she knew of—mostly new
addresses !

G. left us, quite glad, I think, to have made some
contacts down here, and Glyndwr and I went round
the shelled flats with her. Glyndwr is one big Welsh
flirt—yes, indeed ! He knows exceedingly little
German, but he has a rolling eye—Evert was quite

cut out, though I had dutifully conveyed his greetings. . . . She must have a funny idea of the English Labour Party, for, after all, one makes one's generalisations out of particulars, and these particulars are both so young and so very comradely. Glyndwr calls it making direct contact. Anyway, she enjoyed it, so that was all right. There was quite a gay passage when they were trying to discover which had the coldest hands.

When we were in the wrecked flats, it was different. Glyndwr was shocked, as all these post-war children are, and she was grim and sad. Nothing had been done since I had been here last ; there was no word of Government help. In one flat we met the woman it had belonged to, wandering about disconsolately. The flat must have had a superb view out to the west, where now there were no windows, but a great gap torn in the wall. " Es war so schön im roten Wien," she said, and I talked to her a little, but could not say the final *Freundschaft* and *Freiheit*, because two others walked in, and I didn't know if they were really friends.

I wanted Glyndwr to see some of the people, so I told Mrs. T. that I'd give some money to two families. The first was a woman whose husband was in prison, and who had three children. She wore a peasant handkerchief over her head, and talked broad dialect. I impressed on her to say nothing, as Mrs. T. asked me to. She had been living all this time on the charity of neighbours. So had the second, whose husband was also in—she didn't know what sentence he would get, and she had not been allowed to see him yet. She wore a good cloth costume— three guineas, as it were, and a silk scarf knotted round her neck. But now she had nothing. Her flat had all its windows broken, and she'd had to have them mended, as she had a small boy in bed with mastoid. The child was up and about now, a jolly little boy of about seven—but he had a toy gun and he *would* play, " Hands up, or I shoot," and his mother couldn't bear it. But all the children do that. The doctor had told his mother she could pay " when better times came." It must have been pretty wretched for her to accept money, but at least when I gave it I made it clear that it wasn't charity but friendship from the comrades in *Ausland*. If she thought it was the T.U. fund, that didn't matter ; it was probably all to the good.

We went back, for a few minutes, to Mrs. T.'s flat, where she took a cigarette from Glyndwr and then put it away hastily when her mother came in ! I expect it was all fun for both of them. Glyndwr is a very different proposition from Evert. I believe Evert is really nice-minded (and Oxford) and not tough, while Glyndwr is probably naughty-minded (and Cambridge) and fairly tough, though probably not nearly so tough as he would like one to think. He has a nice rolling eye and sings songs in Welsh, which are like West Highland songs in a way, but, instead of sounding as if they were all about mournful maidens, sound oddly indecent. Probably I only think he is a villain because he had a delicious proletarian Welsh voice, like the Welsh villain in my new novel ; he may even be a perfectly pure young man—one never knows. He is fairly simple, though, compared with Evert, who is incredibly complicated and involved, and has all kinds of nerve-strains that no one has a right to have at his age, and which will probably compose themselves in time. When I say he is nice-minded, I mean it almost entirely as a compliment, for *nice* was a good word not so long ago, when it was near to the original *nesh*. I think he has certain decencies which an older person (like me, for instance) tends not to have, and which are absolutely sound until one is completely adult. Up to now, this diary has been passing round fairly freely, but I think this must stop ! That's the worst of getting to know people.

Frau B., the widow of one of the Schutzbund leaders, was to come to see Janet about her pass to England. Evert and I were sent to the interview. I protested, because I disliked the idea of the poor woman being put through it, and so did Evert, but it was no good. Sam also suggested an article I should do, but I convinced him that I wasn't the right person. People who know me as a perfectly ordinary person can't get it into their heads that to a great section of the British public (carefully coached) I am a dangerous and probably wicked woman. I heard afterwards that, this same afternoon, some correspondent was told by a Legation official, at the Press tea, that Naomi Mitchison (whom he suspected was at the back of the two-Englishwomen story) was an irresponsible, dangerous Communist. I suppose they think anyone irresponsible whose heart at all, or ever, counts as against their head. I suspect *The Times* correspondent of being awfully responsible. But the Legation, by the way, were really moved when they heard that one of the Englishwomen was a second cousin of Lord Harewood. Gosh !

Somehow, an incredibly macabre atmosphere had worked itself up for us to meet poor Frau B. in. I have an immense respect for Janet's general courage and ability, and the amount she has managed to find out—she speaks Viennese perfectly—but I can't help feeling she is sometimes a bit of an atrocity-fan. Evert and I waited, both of us tired and hungry, and dreading the interview. Evert managed to evade the first meeting by being busy with the telephone.

Frau B. came in, a tall, strong-looking woman, her face showing the determined shape of the head-bones under it. She was dressed in deep mourning, with a long crape veil, and her strong hands kept on moving and twitching all the time, her fingers twisting at her wedding ring. By her was her doctor, a nice little man in horn spectacles, sitting plumply in his chair, while, she in hers, sat up straight and

hard ; and Janet leant forward, interpreting eagerly ;
and I took notes, trying not to look too like a newspaper woman—every now and then, Frau B. looked
at me with deep distrust, telling Janet that I was
to put nothing into my paper. I saw, almost at once,
that there was no " story " here, and I was very
pleased the real correspondents had not come.

Frau B. is being bothered a good deal by the
police, which is extremely bad for her, and she wants
to get away, with her two small children, to rest for
a time. The Russians offered to have her to stay in
Moscow, where " naturally, she would address
large meetings." She will have to get a job to do
some time soon, for she is that sort of woman, but
probably for a month or so she ought to rest, and,
when she does get a job, it should be doing the kind
of thing that really interests her—work with
children, I gather. She had been quite unpolitical
before this.

She has insisted on her bare rights—her pension
and an education allowance for the children. There
are signs that the Government would like to get hold
of them, and give them a religious education. She
is being watched, and sometimes the police turn up
and question her. She is fierce and anxious, and
very nervous. She kept on biting her lips ; she must
get away.

Evert and I came back, late and hungry. The hotel
people don't seem to like me at all. I wonder if I
ought to tip them more ?—there's ten per cent on

the bill, and I'm so bad at tipping ; it makes me blush ! I'd rather give them a lump sum than small tips, too, but I don't know what the custom is. Conceivably they suspect us—they may all be police spies for all we know. Or they may merely be shocked by everyone coming to my bedroom at all hours. But I don't *think* it's that. These are the moments when one wants a strong silent man to do the tips !

MARCH 12TH

Yesterday we started at 7.15 and didn't get back till 9.30, and I was too tired to write about it. I was at the stage of tiredness when I should just like to have sat still and had someone to make love to me. However there wasn't anyone to do that, so, instead, I had a lovely bath and a sleeping tablet. I tend to have nightmares now, mostly about being chased, or else about being chloroformed, which is rather a bore. Last night I only dreamt about pushing a pram with someone else's baby, but I didn't get such a good sleep as I might, because they woke me early—with letters. But at least the English side is working splendidly—whatever it seems like here ! More money is coming. We have now got to get this end of it clear, which is very difficult, because, the moment one decides one thing, circumstances arise which make another course apparently essential !

Well, on Sunday morning early, Evert, Lisbe, and I caught the express—Evert performing miracles of complicated ticket-buying—and got straight into the dining-car and had breakfast—an excellent thing to do when one is travelling third, as one thus avoids crowds and hard seats ! And there, who should turn up but the *Herald's* Geneva correspondent, whom I had met three days before. He had some fine photographs, and some magnificent stories from Bruck an der Mur—Wallisch's town—how the Heimwehr buried his hanged body by night so that no one should know, but somehow it *was* known, and, after that, for three days the grave was covered with flowers, which the Heimwehr took away every morning. And at last there was a written inscription, " To our Unforgotten Leader," and then the flowers were left.

He had seen the prison there—a cinema full of prisoners, with a machine gun on the stage pointing at them, and Heimwehr patrolling the gallery with bombs ready to throw : a nice cheery atmosphere. The authorities were very angry that he had seen it, though. We sat conspiring, in our horn spectacles, in the restaurant car, and then it was St. Pölten, and Evert, Lisbe, and I got out.

It is a pleasant little town on a Sunday, though the evidence of industrial depression was bad and

185

obvious. There were lots of people in country clothes, though—men in green felt hats, or black hats with green bands or cords, embroidered waistcoats sometimes, and here and there a woman in an embroidered shawl. We made our plans, and went off to see the civil authorities. The heads of the *Bezirk*—a kind of county governor, I suppose, with control over civil and some police forces—interviewed us in a room with mauve and gold wallpaper and a green stove. Evert was the newspaper correspondent who had come to visit prisons, so as to be able to send a *démenti* of the lies about them which had been put across by the Socialists—his colleagues were doing the same thing in other towns. Lisbe was his secretary, industriously taking notes. I was a well-known English writer, and particularly stupid, though indefinitely friendly. Evert did all the talking, and did it superbly ; he might have been the *Morning Post* in person. It was, of course, a perfectly respectable way for a journalist to collect his news, but I wish I could think I would ever be able to lie like that !

Our friend was definitely a nice man ; he had a small head and a large jaw, but the largeness of his jaw was more fat than fierceness, and he was most friendly and helpful, and seemed to be amazingly without political views. He put on an overcoat, and took us along to the *Anhaltelager*, the concentration camp where many of the prisoners were held—probably the least serious cases. As we went out, a man in knickerbockers, with a gun which looked too big

for him, leapt to attention, and here and there
Heimwehr or police saluted, rather awkwardly, like
the frog footman. The Heimwehr here looked a much
better lot than the thin and untidy Viennese troops.
These were fresh-faced country boys, decent looking
on the whole. In some families in the country, the
father and bread winner is a prisoner, and his son
may have to enlist in the Heimwehr so as to bring in
a Schilling or two for the family.

The concentration camp is a large empty factory
(another sign of depression), with a great hall in the
middle, in which there are ninety-one prisoners, all
men ; it has electric lights, water-closets, and quite
good top lighting. They sleep on straw all round
the walls, and have small suitcases, with their own
clothes, rugs, books, etc., and are allowed food from
outside, as well as that which is supplied. There was
a table with dice, cards, etc., on it.

When we came in, they all stood to attention, in
two rows, and grinned at us. Evert walked up and
down, questioning them, always with our friend,
and a Heimwehr officer—very Prussian looking—as
well. I went round with a nice Heimwehr man with
side-whiskers, who didn't seem to frighten them,
though no doubt his presence would make it more
difficult to talk. They all spoke a rather difficult
dialect, and I picked up little except that they complained of the lack of ventilation, especially at night.
Also a lack of pretty girls !—this from a handsome
young man in a blue shirt. I said it was so sad I

couldn't understand German better ; they said, " Ah, but we understand you "—and grinned. But whether this was sex or politics, I am still not sure. They were, on the whole, a very intelligent-looking lot, not, in general, country boys ; some seemed definitely to be intelligentsia, as it were, a local lawyer or chemist or municipal official. Some looked quite incredibly odd—as though they had been arrested for that alone.

Evert talked more, and said that only one man was stopped from speaking to him—when he began to say he was guiltless. They only complained about the air and difficulty of sleeping. Some didn't know why they were there. None of them seemed to know what was going to happen, or what definite charges were to be made against them. They were allowed to see visitors, I gather, rather irregularly, but, as we went out, our conductor told someone, in our presence, that they were to be allowed to see visitors for three-quarters of an hour each.

We were taken on from there to the *Bezirksamt*, all talking very friendlily. This man was obviously a decent sort, and naturally humane. A few in the concentration camp had complained to Evert of their earlier treatment, when they were brought into the small local police-stations, but it didn't look as if there were any complaints here. We had seen the kitchen, and tasted the rice soup and salt pork which they were getting for dinner—they were very proud of their kitchen, and, indeed, it was beautifully

188

clean and efficient-looking. We could compliment our friend sincerely on his camp.

After he left us, we went first to what we were told was the scene of the fighting, but discovered nothing, except that the Heimwehr were now living in the house of the *Kinder-Freunde*. There were no bullet-marks to be seen. We next went to the magistrate's flat, and knocked. We were let into a rather dingy passage, whose principal contents were some two dozen jars of marmalade, an aspidistra, and a douche-can. A girl called her father, and a dear old man came out and looked at us a little suspiciously ; he had a very long smooth white beard, and a brown jacket with frogs and a plaid collar, and woolly boots ; he was the chief magistrate of St. Pölten. He took us through into a room mostly furnished with cacti, bearded like their master ; we apologised profusely for coming on Sunday, and explained again that we were good English journalists come to deny the rumours about prisons.

Thereupon he got his daughter to ring up the prison, and sent us along with his blessing. There are five hundred and sixty men in this prison, of whom four hundred and fifty are Socialists, and a very few women. It is an oldish prison, but there is electric light and efficient central heating, and the windows can be opened. Our magistrate had told us himself that the food was not really sufficient, but it was all the *Regierung* would allow. We verified this. There is meat once a week, on Sundays (this time rather tasteless boiled beef), but not at other times. One of the officials said that this was more than many of them get at home (which is symptomatic of the poverty here). On other days they had occasional vegetables, a lot of potatoes, rice, coffee (fig-coffee probably), ground rice, sago, etc., and a quarter of a loaf—this pale brown, sourish bread—per head per day. They talked about calory values, and no doubt this food is considerably better than, say many unemployed families get in England. But it was certainly deficient in fats and proteins.

In general, the prison was overcrowded. Most cells were meant for two and held four. A few larger cells were meant for ten, and held about thirty—this was much the same in Leoben, which M. visited. The work cells were also occupied, and there were four men in the *Krankenzelle*, or it might have been six, who had been beaten, and three of whom had been shot with dum-dum bullets, after arrest by the police or *Hilfs-Polizei*—the Heimwehr. This had always happened at the beginning in the smaller towns of which St. Pölten is the centre.

The procedure was this : we were taken round by two officials, one of whom spoke a little English, and a warder who opened the cells and shouted *Achtung*, at which the men inside sprang to attention, and were on their feet staring at us when we got to the cell ourselves. The men wore their own clothes, an odd assortment, often no boots, and one could see that in civil life they had mostly been workers or

small professional people. Each cell had rolled
mattresses, one or two chairs, and a small table, on
which their books were, games and papers. Of course
these were Government papers, and served as
propaganda ; foreign papers were not allowed—but
we never discovered anyone who spoke English or
French, though we asked several times. They were
allowed to smoke. When we got to a cell, Evert went
in first, saying we were foreign journalists ; then Lisbe
went in with her note-book, as secretary, and then I
talked hard, in bad and difficult German, to the
prison official, so that he should have his work cut
out to understand and answer me, and shouldn't
overhear what was being said—actually I heard
very little myself, and I think a man could probably
have spoken to Evert fairly easily without being
overheard. The other two officials stayed outside.

I must say, at once, I thought the head official,
with whom we went round, was a very decent sort of
man, with a humane face and sane instincts. The
other official seemed all right, and so did the
warders. I didn't think the prisoners looked frightened of them. It was rather horrible, but, then,
prisons are. I don't think it was made any worse
than it might have been by any of the officials
concerned.

Evert spoke to men in a number of cells, and
gathered a fair general idea of the conditions. The
complaints of present treatment were that no
visitors were allowed ; theoretically they might have

been, by the magistrate, but actually they weren't. People were not allowed food packets, either, though relatives might bring clean clothes and, apparently, flowers. But the worst thing was that many had not been investigated at all, their cases had not even been stated, they did not know what they were to be charged with, and they had got no legal advice or help (this can only be given after the charge-sheet is formulated). Remember, these people had been in prison for almost four weeks already. There is nothing corresponding to habeas corpus, and there seemed no reason to suppose their cases would come up by any given date.

As far as cruelty is concerned, many complained to Evert of beatings and maimings at the *gendarmerie* —the local small police-stations, either by police or Heimwehr ; one had a finger off ; others had crushed feet ; one said he had been so beaten he could not sleep for three weeks. But none complained of any ill-treatment since they had been in prison.

All of them were terribly worried about their wives and children ; they said they would be all right if only they knew that their families were not on the street. They got no news of them.

They did not complain particularly of the over-crowding, but it must have been pretty bad ; they only had an hour's exercise a day, in an incredibly dreary prison-yard. Otherwise they were all on top of one another. No doubt it is better than "solitary," but it reminded me rather of old Newgate conditions.

Many of them were very young—in one of the groups
of thirty there was a sixteen-year-old boy.

The Nazis were imprisoned separately, again
mostly in large groups, and overcrowded. But they
had all had their charges formulated, and were
already serving their sentences, which were mostly
six weeks, the longest three months. We asked them
what for. They said for shouting " Heil Hitler," or,
" Down with the Bundes-Kanzler " (" The *Herr*
Bundes-Kanzler " corrected our official, and everyone laughed). What struck me immediately was the
difference in spirits between the two. The Nazis
were all quite cheery, the Socialists all pretty
miserable and depressed. They say they are separated
so that they should not fight, but Evert suggested that
this is so as to keep the Nazi propaganda from the
depressed Socialists.

In the women's cell there were two political
prisoners among some six or eight ordinary criminals.
One woman had been arrested because of having
had Social Democrats in her house. Her husband
was a perfectly respectable ticket-collector, and had
briefed a lawyer to advise her. But she had not been
allowed to see either the lawyer or her husband
since her arrest three-and-a-half weeks before.
Another woman said : " They say I handed grenades
to the Schutzbund," which was obviously true, and
of which she was obviously proud. She didn't mind
saying it in front of the officials, either. Here, again,
the charge-sheets had never been formulated, and

bail seems hardly ever to be given to the political prisoners.

While this was going on, I talked in the other part of the cell (it was a big, double cell, with a sewing-machine, plants in pots and so on) to one of the other women. She said she was in for eight months but had been in for two before her case came up ; she was only allowed to see her husband once in three weeks, and wasn't allowed to see her children at all. She was a nice woman, I thought ; I didn't like to ask her what she was in for—I think she liked seeing me, and was interested in my fur collar. She said that the chief official was a *guter Mensch*—this was denied by one of the others, but she was definitely rather odd ; I think she was in for soliciting. I'm inclined to think mine was a thief. We all said " *Grüss Gott* " very friendlily at the end.

We were taken to see the chapel, the prison-yard, and the prison pigs, of which the official was very proud—they provided him with a margin for his diet —he could give his prisoners sausage and blood-soup occasionally ; the warder scratched the pigs' ears affectionately. Several men looked out of the windows and waved to us. " That is forbidden," said the official, but smiled at us when we waved back.

We were then very tired—it took some time—so, after good-byes and thank-yous (and I feel that when people behave decently, one should give them credit for that and say so to their faces—for that's one side of propaganda), we went towards the railway station.

194

Evert had a fantastic scheme for going on to Linz and seeing all the prisons there in three hours, but I was a little discouraging and insisted that we should see the man of whom I had heard from Janet. We went to his address, where they said, firmly, that he was not there, having very nearly denied that he existed ; but we thought he was probably there all the same, so we tried to explain, tactfully, who we were, and said when we should be at the railway station. Then we lunched, hoping vainly that it would buck us up.

When we went to the station, we found the young man—not much more than a boy. We all went to a café, but the waiter insisted on coming and reading a newspaper, leaning over a table beside us. We sent for more coffee, and took his newspaper away, but he brought another and read it ! However, in intervals, and again outside, we got some information from him. Our friend told us we had not seen the police prison, and drew us a map of where it was. He also told us of three people who had been badly beaten up (one had been shot in the feet by a dum-dum bullet, and had lost one foot) and were in the hospital.

So off we went to the hospital, but found there that we could not see the young men without special permission, and in the presence of a policeman ; one of them had not yet seen any relative, but his mother was to come the next day. I believe he was under twenty. We could not get the permit in time, and anyhow could not have got much with it ; besides it mightn't have been very good for the invalids.

Then we determined to try the police prison. Remember, very few prisons have so far been seen, either by journalists or by relief workers, and we were prepared for a rebuff here. The other officials whom we had seen had not definitely said in so many words that theirs were the only prisons, but they had certainly implied it.

We went to the police-station—in a most lovely fifteenth-century building, with carving over the lintels and a great red, high-pitched roof—in a square with a nice, silly baroque monument in the middle. We waited there, in a room full of rifles, while a policeman telephoned ; they were all most polite. After a time he said we must find the head man (who is—or is also—I gather, head of the Heimwehr). We went across to the little local theatre, where they were doing an operetta, and we waited in the *foyer*, looking at signed photographs of third-rate tenors, and wondering how to work it. By and bye a Prussian-looking official *en civile* came down. Evert, like a good journalist, was prepared for all methods, but started by being very polite ; if he could do it by smiling through, all the better.

But, most surprisingly, our Prussian said, yes, that would be all right, if we didn't mind going round with the police sergeant, as he was in the middle of his operetta. So again, with goodwill on both sides,

196

we parted. The policeman took us through a courtyard—all the houses were old and rather beautiful
—and into the police prison. It was older, and more
uncomfortable and primitive than the other prison,
but there was electric light and some kind of central
heating. Here, again, the overcrowding was bad—
four to a cell which would only take two as a crowd.
The sergeant seemed more suspicious of Evert
talking, though I tried the same tactics. But here
again the same complaints of no charge having yet
been made, and of beatings and mishandlings early
on by the local *gendarmerie*. Nothing else, and
they looked all right. I gather food was much the
same.

I noticed on the wall the Three Arrows, in pencil
(in the corridor, not a cell), and asked the policeman, innocently, what it was. He said, " Oh, the
Social Democrats make that," but seemed uncon-
cerned. We went into one or two cells full of Nazis
and found they had scribbled swastikas and " Heil
Hitlers " all over them. Again one noticed the
difference between the cheerfulness of the Nazis
and the gloom of the Socialists.

We went into a courtyard beyond (in this courtyard, we had been told, there had been a couple of
hundred men and women, sleeping out, with only
two blankets apiece for the women, nothing for the
men, and only let out when they gave names—we
saw no signs of that, but the policeman told us they
had had more prisoners up to a few days ago). At

the back of the courtyard was another small prison. Here, in one very dark cell—the windows with a grating over them—were some fifteen or so men. They were, however, also allowed in the corridor— the door was not locked. While Evert and the sergeant were in another smaller cell, I went quickly to this, and asked them how things were ; I was alone, and obviously friendly, and if there had been anything to say they could have said it—if they'd had their wits about them. And again, when Evert and Lisbe and the sergeant were in this cell, I stood in the passage, where the sergeant couldn't see me, and nodded to one of the men to come out and talk. However, he didn't. And again, when they were in the third small cell, I went back to this one, and again was alone for a moment. So I believe that if anything dreadful had been happening which they were afraid to speak of, they might have managed to get it across to me.

In the big cell was one man who was going on hunger-strike the next day. His son was one of the boys in hospital, and he hadn't been allowed to see him ; he had applied again and again, and finally was arrested. He himself was quite unpolitical. Here, again, there were complaints of former beatings, but all looked pretty well.

Coming out in the yard, people waved to us from the windows, and the sergeant tactfully looked away. Next he showed us two empty rooms, in which, he said, strangers coming through the town, and spending a night in it, could sleep. They were given supper and breakfast, and had to tidy it up before they started off. This seems more humane than the English work system.

He then asked if we wouldn't like to see all over the police-station, and showed us their marvellous card-index, all very German, of all the people and all the houses of St. Pölten—showing us the cards with particulars on one side, and police strafes on the other. He showed his own—beautifully blank ! It was a magnificent old building, built round two squares. I looked out of the window, trying to spot any possible prison windows in the rest of the building, but most were either unbarred or had lace curtains. It is possible he was hiding something, but I very much doubt it. I must say that this sergeant, too, seemed a very decent man.

We then went back to the young man, who seemed disappointed that we had seen nothing worse, and gave us two facts. One, that people were being kept in concentration camps until their employers had to dismiss them. Two, that lawyers who undertake the defence of a group of Socialists have their title to practise taken from them. And, of course, there are not nearly enough to go round if men are to be defended singly. However, this must be verified. He also said that no help of any kind was being given in St. Pölten.

By this time we were all incredibly tired. I was going to sleep over my note-book, Lisbe was wilting like a blonde daisy, only Evert remained polite ; at last we said good-bye, and slid and slumped down the stairs into the street, there to find we had inexorably to wait an hour and a half for the next train. We bought cakes at a shop ; they were frightfully good cakes, and we were hungry, but somehow we were too tired to enjoy them. We went to a café, and tried to cheer up and talk scandal about our friends. Lisbe tells me the Adlerian psycho-analysts who try to root out religion are going to have a bad time, and that one eminent she-professor is being told she must resign. Evert ordered some beer, on the grounds that people who were as tired as he was always order beer and enjoy it, but he didn't. Then he called me an old dear, and I nearly cried, it made me feel so nearly forty ! And, God knows, I looked it after that day ! I decided to wash my hair as soon as possible.

At last the train turned up, and we pushed one another into it, and we ate an omelette, so as to be able to sit in the restaurant-car on soft seats, and by and bye we arrived, and I fell asleep to the sound of Evert across the way being telephoned to by another correspondent.

This morning came all the Saturday papers, with the " Two Englishwomen Arrested " story. The *Express* had it best, I think—if you like their methods. Poor Lass was made to talk about her Little One, just like James Douglas. Some of them had got across all the things they'd been wanting to get for an age.

The Times was poor, and the *Morning Post* worse. The *Daily Mail* put "stated that" before everything, so as to make it look improbable. And, incidentally, there are the election results ! The jolly old L.C.C.— I'm wondering if I shall see Gemeinde Hauser all over London when I get back ! I spent part of the morning discussing things with Sam and the others, and part of it mending my typewriter, which seems almost to want psycho-analysing. Lunch with various comrades, on and off, then more talk with Sam, which at least clarified my own views, and helped me to see how money ought to be spent. People have at last come from Transport House ; they have to be chased and talked to, they won't come of themselves, for, after all, we are Dangerous and Irresponsible, as the Legation also said, and tainted with a university education and all that. But, according to to-day's letters, the home front are co-operating magnificently. I think the journalistic side of all this is now going to be dealt with by the professionals, so I shall have nothing to do but sit back and criticise.

Then I came back—and washed my hair, and I hope I look a bit less like an Old Dear ! Since then I've been writing hard, and trying to make out my accounts, which are excessively puzzling, since some are in Schillings and others in pounds, and I can't remember which are which. I am still wondering whether I can get that embroidered jersey—if only I could think of a good-enough excuse ! By the way,

I noticed one perfume shop in the town, which says it is an Arian establishment which wishes only Arian customers. I wonder if that pays?

MARCH 13TH

This morning I was going to meet Mrs. T. at Lass's flat; she was to bring addresses. I was just going off to meet her, when Lass rang up to say that she thought there was a plain-clothes man standing just inside the big door. At that, Glyndwr and I dashed off in a taxi. I went up while Glyndwr waited for my girl-friend (with whom he had got on to quite good terms at Floridsdorf! so it wasn't too hard on him). However, I saw no plain-clothes man, and finally decided it was all right. Glyndwr went off to consult about legal defence, and Mrs. T. turned up, looking as pretty and gay as ever. She has, of course, done nothing which is not perfectly legal and proper, but she wanted to warn us about the talking which is going on—anything from gossip to real treachery. She says that, within an hour or two of Lass's arrest, it was all over Floridsdorf. We discussed the legal position. Most of it was old news— foreigners not allowed in the Austrian courts— though several had approached the authorities.

No Socialist lawyers to be had, and others won't take the cases. And so on. We discussed the family next door, and I took her off to see a man who might, I hoped, be able to help her over this. However, he tried two lawyers while I was there, neither of whom would help, though they were sympathetic. Eighty per cent of the Viennese Bar are Jews, and, of course, they are terrified to do anything, standing, as they are, between one set of Nazis and another. He gave me another possible address.

The evening before, Glyndwr had discussed the legal position with certain other people. But, of course, one difficulty is that he and Sam and all of us are highbrows with Oxford (or Cambridge) accents. However, various people have come out from England on various errands, and I don't think I need do any more journalism unless it really comes my way.

I asked Mrs. T. to come back and have lunch with me—first she refused, then said she would. She tells me she's a milliner by profession, and she would love to make something for me. I should love her to, but I don't quite know what to suggest. We walked back, looking in at all the shop-windows, giggling when we met anyone with particularly funny clothes, and deciding it was nice to be friends. She said how much she'd like a sister. And between times, cautiously, we talked politics—she says, and it's true of course : " We missed our time." She also told me of rows in Floridsdorf between police and Heimwehr.

I gave her a copy of the *Outline*, and she gave me a fountain-pen, made by her cousin, at his works. I think she found the lunch rather embarrassing—all the young men turned up, and, of course, it's a large and fairly elaborate place—not very expensive (the menu is 2.50), but definitely unproletarian. She blushed a lot, but I think she liked it. It was fun for me, anyway.

I tried to tell her something about my life—the house in Hammersmith, from here so ridiculously large and full of people—Oxford—the children—Dick. But I don't think I conveyed much, nor, probably, does it matter to our relationship that I didn't. What does matter is that one has somehow dug a little channel for the sweet waters of international friendship and goodwill ; she, and to some extent her children and friends, will now think of England rather differently. And, goodness knows, we need to make them do that—after the Treaty of Versailles. She told me of their war generation—tired, as ours was. They could not—physically could not—take the chance of Socialism that there was in the troubled times after the war ; they were too tired for any more risks. So things went back into the hands of the generation before them, as with us. And now ?

Then, in the curious way things occur here, Anne turned up again. She was dead tired, her whole face drooping with tiredness, and yet underneath was the glow, the aliveness, which makes her such a special person, which means that she lives not only in her intellect—which is impressive enough—but through the *praxis* of personal relationships. I suppose any new, re-stated, Socialist Party must for a time depend quite a lot on this sort of *praxis*, which is a long way from representational government—the thing we are used to think of as democracy—but is perhaps near to the original democracy of the fifth century. We talked for a time, then she left me, and, for the next several hours, Glyndwr and I worked on the report for England on the state of the law here, I typing from his dictation or his semi-legible notes, and occasionally altering things. He has been verifying things—so often one's first information or impression is wrong. For instance, it is *not* true that Socialist lawyers are arrested for defending groups of Socialists, but one of them has been, apparently for doing this, and the others are afraid of it, so the effect tends to be the same. We cannot find out for certain when the trials are coming on—some people say quite soon, others not till summer. It is perfectly clear—and made doubly so by our this morning's experience in trying to find a lawyer for poor Frau F—— S——, that there will not conceivably be enough lawyers to defend the thousands of cases now awaiting trial. The leaders will probably be all right and their cases will be sufficiently important for the best lawyers to take them, and probably make a fine show out of them, but what about all the poor unhappy Schutzbundlers and their friends and relations, all these hundreds and hundreds of obscure men and women in Vienna, and all over Austria, who can't afford a great blaze of attack, who must be defended with alibis and denials, and be allowed to go back to their homes with at least a possible chance of finding work again—and living?

What has to be done at present is to defend the Austrian Bar and Bench against Government pressure. There are plenty of fine lawyers and judges whose integrity cannot be called into question, but the Dollfuss Government has cleverly altered procedure, and is putting pressure, direct and indirect, to bear on the whole system of justice. That is the kind of thing where outside influence can help. If we had a good Foreign Secretary—a real Liberal, even—instead of Simon, things might be easier. Odd to think he is a lawyer, too, who certainly once used to care for justice.

Glyndwr and I had a slight pause for tea—I make tea most evenings on my little stove, but only highbrow tea with lemon; milk is too complicated! Another pause while I went out and bought more typing paper; again a pause, for dinner. We decided that it would be nice to go out, when it was all finished, and hear some music, or even dance. But when we went over to Sam's with it—for it has to go off to England to-morrow, worn next the heart, or in the knickers, by one of our " travellers " —we discovered that we had gone wrong on certain small matters of fact. It is fearfully difficult to get all that quite accurate, but absolutely essential to do so. The others were there—poor dears, it was ten o'clock, and they'd had nothing to eat since lunch—and Glyndwr sat down to rewrite it.

The corrections were made, but by that time it was 11.30 ; Glyndwr and I, after starting off towards a café, suddenly felt too tired even to listen to music, still less to observe or participate in the night-life of Vienna ! So we came back, and I made more tea, and he and I and Evert, in an interval of writing his despatch for Scotland, talked. I am always afraid of shocking those two boys. I am beginning to suspect that Glyndwr is really a nice young man too, in spite of his shop-window of the tough Welsh proletarian. They're both such dears, and I suspect they've both got to go through hell before they grow up, before they can cease being individualists. For they realise intellectually that one mustn't be, that one can't begin to lead the good life while one is, but, before any man or woman can really do that, he or she must somehow or other be put through the mangle. I expect these two have got to be hurt, and made to feel worthless and alone, and generally pulled to pieces ; and they've got to accept it too, not struggle against it, and then they can build up again, into a different kind of existence in which they will have accepted and been accepted by some community—something with bigger and more beautiful and less easily understandable standards and values than the individualist ones. And, of course, they may in this process be broken and be unable to accept, and then they're done for as useful human beings (unless, conceivably, they can be put together by some artificial process such as psycho-therapy). Or, of course, it mayn't ever happen—as it doesn't happen to lots and lots of people, who stay contented individualists to the end of their lives (which, for them, *is* the end). But I believe it probably will happen to these two, especially perhaps to Glyndwr, whose tough outside conceivably holds a rather tender inside, and who realises that he is compromising and lying to himself. When a Celt has this experience, and ceases to lie to himself in the way Welsh and Irish and Highlanders do normally, then he may turn into something rather powerful. But it's going to be pain to them both. During this process, you need a good deal of plain, honest kindness from other people. I'm probably too old, too out of their generation, to be much use to either of them, but I hope they'll find someone.

These last two days have been odd. Up to the end of last week there was a constant strain and pressure —one was so immersed in action that one had no time to recede from the heights. Now things have changed. Instead of active work, we have co-ordination to do, keeping touch with people, not all of whom are in agreement, thinking things out, not for the immediate and dangerous next hour or two— at the most to-morrow and the day after—but for months ahead. I am already making plans for

England—and what will all this seem like when one gets back? What sort of fantastic nightmare? I wish I could sleep without dreaming of it, without waking up in the middle of a plan or a letter, which takes minutes to dissipate and stream away and allow sleep to return.

MARCH 14TH

A calmish morning. Some little talk with Sam, and a lot of gossip with Evert over a late breakfast. The most restful thing one does here is to gossip— or to mend one's stockings. In the middle of it all I came across a young Scots musician one evening at Ian's ; he had a curious accent, half German and half West Coast, and we discussed Hugh M'Diarmid, and for a quarter of an hour everything calmed down to a different, a Hebridean, *tempo*. Evert and I have a lot of friends in common, and, so much more entertainingly, many enemies !

We were to meet V., of the *Manchester Guardian*, at lunch—we had all been so thrilled to hear that the great V. was coming out—so when I turned up at a café and saw a gentle, untidy, snub-nosed man, I said, " Are you V.? " He struck me immediately as having something academic about him, perhaps faintly disapproving—I wasn't sure. Sam and Janet came, and we all four went off to lunch at a small quiet place.

And then V. began to make us all miserable, especially me—at least I thought so till this evening I realised that it had been just as bad for the other two, but Janet had been silenced, while Sam's politeness had never given out. V. explained to us that there was no terror now (as indeed we realised—no terror in the newspaper sense, the " war stories " are over), and that it has never been a terror compared with the German one, as indeed we realised too. He went on to tell us of the Polish terror in the Ukraine—which he had made into big news for the world—when the peasants of a whole country were systematically beaten up ; of the Nazi terror in Germany, and how it still goes on, so that already this year hundreds have been killed and tortured ; of beating-up by the Paris police and the American police ; of how he himself had been beaten—oh, a horrid story. He says that the Paris workers are arming over the heads of their leaders—and the Right are arming as well, and no doubt more competently. And then he said, as Dell has said, that this came of allowing Germany to rearm. Sam and I murmured some faint Lib.-Lab. protests about equality, about Italy, but V. swept on. The world was going Fascist—it was now only possible to live decently on the westward fringes ; he spoke of his English village, and the problem of the Crack in the

Church Bell. Socialism, he said, was dead, the only hope now was in the young Nazis and Fascists. Let us not delude ourselves by talk about Socialism. Everywhere was dictatorship. The express trains of Fascism and Communism tearing towards the Final Day. He would not admit that Russia was different ; he said we were blind. He only saw the express trains as like-formed devils of speed and violence. It made no difference to him that one was going towards and another going away from—what ? We couldn't completely answer him ; one can only see round one corner at a time.

And then he spoke of the things on which Western civilisation as we know it are based, what he called Græco-Roman, but I, at least I think so, would call Greek : all that we mean by Athens. He said that this was going, was being overwhelmed by a Nazi Dark Age. I said no, it was not going, but it must be re-stated. We did not understand it ; we only saw it through the eyes of the prosperous, the historians of a generation ago : now it must be told again, and if we realise that, for instance, fifth-century democracy was bloody and tyrannous, with its bosses and party purges and corruption—but they *did* build the Parthenon, and they *did* give first prizes to Aristophanes—then we could correlate it to our own time, and it would not be despised in Russia. He said that there was a total neglect of these values in Russia. He talked of pure research. I said that at least their genetics were good enough, and I believed their mathematics were. Sam put the Marxist case. But we were all somehow stunned and horrified. It was as though he had taken the lid off hell, like the fifteenth-century German painters did. It made me feel sick. If this is all there is—if our idea of brotherhood and equality is to go down before the Nazis—well, why not go home? Why not buy dresses in Vienna instead of taking money to Florids- dorf? Why wear ourselves out struggling? Why be in danger? If after the manner of men we have fought with beasts at Ephesus, what advantageth it us if the dead rise not? Let us eat, drink, and be merry, for to-morrow we die, whether it is the Nazis who get us or something else.

I went back to the hotel, and into Glyndwr's room, and he said, " I've been looking for you every- where ; I want sixty Schillings." And I sat down on his bed and began to cry, and said, " V. has made me feel as if nothing was worth while." And then he said, " Forty lawyers in Vienna have agreed to defend the Socialists." And then I thought, But the dead will rise—not the individual dead, but the dead, the sodden lump of mankind—that will and must rise, it will take the leaven. Forty just men have been found. Because of forty lawyers in Vienna, it is all right ; and, because this Welshman is a com- rade, it is all right. Even if it is true that the Dark Ages have come back, we cannot stand away in isolation ; just because other people are a good sort of people, because we happen to like them, we've got to stand by them. Taking it at its most hedonistic, we can't be happy unless other people are ; we have to be kind to one another. Glyndwr was kind to me then, and I took it for granted, as one should between comrades ; he was not elaborately kind, but he was what I needed—he gave the sense of *praxis* in personal relationships. Also, he understood, as the English don't understand, this terrible religious sense which is continuously moulding one's forms of thought ; he knows what it's like to go down on one's knees before the universe and say, " Thy will be done," and get from that the sense of atonement. And he knows how one must be strict with oneself, too strict to allow of any redeemer—Jesus or Lenin or Wallisch or Weissl ; one has to go through it all by oneself, although in the company of the *Genossen*, the comrades.

I think this would sound silly to anyone English. As for me, I have the Kirk a generation back—further back still, John Knox, beaten up in the galleys—and Glyndwr was Chapel till three years ago, and now neither of us are even vaguely deists. But the forms and the words are familiar to us. A century ago, in the dark times after the Napoleonic wars, the hungry 'forties, this man and I would have prayed together. As it was, we discussed Marxism ; but there's nothing in that but a difference of time. No, there *is* a difference. One way is looking out at a reflection of oneself in the empty skies ; the other way is looking inward at mankind, and the

laws that govern the thoughts and action of men.
But the intensity of looking, though not the same
way, has the same effect on the soul.

For a little time I went down and talked to Evert
and a friend of his—a gloomy, intelligent man—
about Social Democracy, and whether it was
inevitable that it should not be able to act when the
time comes. He has seen it in America and Germany
and here—always failing ; will it ever be able to
produce leaders who can really lead, not only in
ordinary times, but at times of crisis ? Or does the
machinery of democracy prevent this ? I think myself
that this again is a case for the re-statement of
democracy.

Then I went out with Glyndwr, and, for about an
hour, we chased a young lawyer, from one address
to another—the difficulty being that he has a not
uncommon name ! One gets very good at climbing
endless stairs. At last we found him, a solid, intelligent young Socialist, not a Jew. We discussed the
situation, which is not too bad. The young lawyers
who are undertaking this work (most of them are
young) are taking the cases for a fee of fifty Schillings
(a case may, of course, be settled out of court, but
at the same time, it may last for weeks). We asked
him what he thought of things, and he cited cases of
beating-up, out of the *Manchester Guardian Weekly* !
Inevitably they are out of touch themselves ; it is not
safe for them to be in touch. He seemed amused
about Lass and Lisbe—knew all about it ! And

finally, supposing us to be a married couple, made Glyndwr not only blush, but subsequently stand me some chocolates on the way back—and a bunch of violets at dinner.

Janet took me to see a woman who is running a kind of children's kindergarten. She had various stories, not completely substantiated, about children being taken from various Socialist schools and homes, which have been closed, and put into Catholic schools, but she asked me to wait to write about them until she had verified them. I was glad to do so, for one doesn't always find people having enough regard for accuracy. She also gave me a copy of a very curious children's book, which is being shown in all the shop windows and widely reviewed. It is called *Es wird heilige Kinder geben*, and it is a collection of stories about children who have lived—lately—holy lives and died holy deaths. Every single one of the stories ends in a deathbed, usually with bluggy details, all mixed up with Jesus and Heaven. Pretty disgusting, really, and extremely political. Personally I mind its politics less than I mind the effect of all those foul deathbed scenes on decent children. It seems rather symptomatic of what is going to happen. Even the book-mark was a prayer.

She also gave me certain definite figures. Forty-five Socialist headmasters and mistresses have already been dismissed. At the Spital der Stadt Wien and Karolinen Kinder Spital, all Jewish doctors have been dismissed. Most of the clinics take on their doctors, by agreement, year to year ; now, no more Jews will be taken on. They will have no further prospects of hospital practice. So *silly*.

After that I came back and had dinner with the boy-friends, who were perhaps just faintly cross with one another. Glyndwr gave me the violets. . . . Then I did diary, and Evert came, after his bath, and had tea, and talked to me about grand opera, which was really great fun, as I don't know the first thing about it, and it was like listening to a foreign language, or, rather, looking at a foreign country. He also told me what a nuisance he thought I was going to be before I came, and how he thought I would be all Blooms-bury and have pyjama-parties (which remark came ill from him in his blue and white stripes and after-bath-ishness). I wonder whether the hotel think I'm hopelessly bad, or merely English ? I really don't mind at all.

Then I wrote some more, and then Glyndwr came in, all triumphant and glorious, because the law thing is working out nicely. He has seen the French and Belgian representatives, and he is feeling grand ! His sentences got superbly Welsh and proletarian and tipped up at the end, and the grace of the Lord was with him ! I was so glad he was getting the sense of Vienna at last. It looks rather like his going to Graz, and I think I'd better go with him if he does ; these last three days have, on the whole, been a waste of time for me—and, at the same time, not much rest, for one fidgets, wanting things to do, wanting one's *praxis*.

Dick has written me a letter, which is so obscure—*such* a crossword puzzle—that I can't understand it. Actually, I very much doubt whether any of our incoming letters are tampered with, though our outgoing ones certainly have been found to be from time to time, and all telephone calls are liable to be overheard—those with foreign countries are always listened in to—and telegrams are always looked at, and may be censored. There is, apparently, the hell of a row going on about our visit to St. Pölten, and there'll be no more prison-visiting allowed. Rather silly of them, for, on the whole, St. Pölten was better than we had expected. Glyndwr says that the French lawyer tells him that the *affaire* of the *deux Anglaises* has had a *très grand effet sur le Gouvernement !*

MARCH 15TH: MORNING

The weeklies have come at last. Nothing in the *New Statesman*, to whom I sent the Ottakring story (the direct statement of one of the men, which seemed to me far more impressive than any write-up I could do), except, " There are also tales of horrors in the prisons. . . . We are loath to believe that these brutalities are going on. . . ." Yes, I should think

they were. Damn' loath ! Bloody loath ! Loath !
What a word ! What a nice calm word for editors
to use in nice peaceful legal London ! Nothing in
Time and Tide, to whom I sent a description of
Floridsdorf, all first hand, except a letter from
some Viennese saying the exact opposite and a mild
editorial comment about the Crisis in Austria ! Well,
one answers the letter. But it's annoying when I
consider how I sweated over the stuff that first week ;
how I wrote it when I was dropping with tiredness—
and it wasn't bad stuff either, as writing. These dear
little papers that are willing to call one a genius
when one's writing fiction—words that they don't
need to take action about—but won't have anything to do with one when one's writing something
that really matters ! One sees this highbrow fame
for the hollow, tinny thing it is, when I can't even
get an article of first-rate topical interest published
in a London weekly. Well, I must take them to
the others. I'm ashamed that I couldn't help.
Damn !

MARCH 18TH

This is a bad gap, but the two days since I wrote—
no, just about three days—have perhaps settled in
my memory. There were moments that I don't think

218

I could have put down immediately after they happened ; one was too much part of them to be able to stand away and be even as mildly objective as a diarist must be. Now they have settled in my mind, and I have full pencil notes to write from.

Well, then, to go back to the time I stopped writing, the 15th. I was angry all that morning, stupidly angry. I couldn't bear that someone in an English paper should say these things, even though it was an Austrian writing. I felt ashamed that my Austrian friends should see that letter printed in an English paper. During the morning, I wrote an answer to it, trying not to be as violent as I felt, but necessarily writing with angry adrenalin in my blood-stream, jerking at the nerves of hand and face, clouding the brain. I wonder if there will be other answers to that letter ?—perhaps. My letter to *The Times*, about Amery's speech, was, of course, not published, even though I had made it so tactfully mild, going over it afterwards to subtract any non-*Times* remarks !

I was writing the letter at Sam's, and every now and then someone would come in with news or rumours, and, for a time, one talked. The French and Belgian members of the International Legal Commission were said to be going by car to Graz ; there would be room for me as well as Glyndwr. I thought this would be lovely ; the drive across the mountains would wash the bitterness out of my mind. Then came rumours of what was happening, how the scheme for taking Socialist children out of the country, to Czecho-Slovakia and Switzerland, was being sabotaged by the authorities, partly on straight political grounds, and partly on religious grounds (though it is impossible to separate them), for no doubt the devout Catholics dislike the idea of children crossing the frontier, away from their influence, to fall under that of Protestants or Marxists. One gets the feeling that, as in the Middle Ages, the Church prefers to save souls, even if that means the irreparable damage of minds and bodies. Well—that makes a fundamental cleavage at once. One cannot even argue.

There was news, too, that the workshops, and general organisation for relief, which the Quakers— here largely helped by A. W. and M.—had established at Graz, had been shut down, though later this turned out to be only temporary, as the Dollfuss - Innitzer fund wants to do everything its own way. The Quaker organisation was bothered and anxious, and did not quite know what to do. I have said little about the Quaker organisation here, since I have had little personal contact with it. Though it took a maddeningly long time to get under way, largely because it did not know for certain about money, and though some of its members have had what appeared to me, at least, to have been over-scrupulous consciences, it has finally settled down to work in a grand and thorough way. It has had very great difficulties, as the Government has been extremely suspicious of its activities, and it has never known for certain whether some piece of work which it has undertaken might not be suddenly stopped, or taken over by the devout : which tends to mean the same thing. And, of course, there were certain pieces of work which it could not touch. The whole thing has been quite astonishingly unpolitical—the Quaker mentality, perhaps alone among social mentalities, allows for that. It is, of course, for that reason that I have had nothing to do with them, beyond handing over lists of names of people who could be non-politically helped, and were not afraid of having their names " *bei den Quäkern*." The Quaker organisation could not—quite rightly—have let me have anything to do with them. I should only have increased their anxiety. I cannot personally work in that way, nor quite agree with their principles, but admire them more the more I see of them.

Well, then, we went back to lunch at the hotel ; Anne was there, laughing at me for being so angry, so English ! So were several others. Grace has come, and is establishing contacts quickly. Before I was through with my first course, Glyndwr turned up, and it was a case of getting the legal report typed out. He also said that the car wasn't going after all, but we looked up a good train, about seven.

That afternoon was real hell. I don't mind working against time myself on my own job, but this was different. I didn't know the stuff, so Glyndwr had to write it, and he's not practised as I am, so he

had to hack out the sentences, with worrying and
pain, for me to type. It appeared that we would
have to have six copies, which is more than my
Corona can take. At first I had C., but he is a slow
typist—it's maddening to work with anyone slower
than oneself—however, then Gert's sister turned up.
She is the least showy person of all ; when the rest
of us are swanking, or having hysterics or rushing
round in circles, she cooks meals and types, and
refuses to consider herself as a heroine, and is nice
to everyone ; she is a splendidly quieting and nice
person to be with. Now she did the duplicating
from my corrected sheets. The room got strewn with
paper. I dashed into Glyndwr's room every few
minutes, and hung over him impatiently while he
did the stuff—like a printer's devil waiting for
copy. He began to look more and more dishevelled
with the effort—his hair stood on end. Sometimes I
made suggestions, or even stylistic alterations, but,
in general, he wrote very clearly, and in the right
way. He got his facts and figures clear ; most of
them had been twice verified.

In the middle of all this, we had to dash off and
meet V. of the *Manchester Guardian*, also our G., who
is, in general, good uncle to all of us. V. was still
very depressing, but yet I think he'll write good
stuff. I hardly know what it is, but Glyndwr ex-
perienced just my misery—that what V. says is
true, and yet, although true, it is not, to my mind,
valid for action. It is a kind of academic truth.

Glyndwr and I, both being university bred, felt it come down on us as though from a respected professor—all the worse for his being obviously such a nice man.

Another interruption was towards the end—when we had irrevocably missed the good train. We had to give our stuff to Mr. G—— to take back. I like both Mr. G—— and Mr. P., and I don't think they disliked or mistrusted me. Both these two are non-academic people of action. Their ways of wasting time are rather different to mine, but it all comes to much the same thing in the long run.

Well, the report got finished—I stiff all up my arms, from rapid typing ; Glyndwr exhausted. We packed rucksacks. It seemed on the cards that we might be going towards possible arrest, so everything dangerous—addresses and so on—had to be moved out of my room.

We had a hasty meal, and went off, with not much more than time to catch the train. The thirds were mostly packed, but at last we found two seats, one in a corner, and put down our rucksacks. Then we came out again, and stood in the corridor while the big train drew out of Vienna, the house- and street-lights gradually spacing and scattering as we passed through the southern suburbs, while, gradually too, it became clear that the sky was full of wild stars. It was now past ten o'clock. The train was going south-west—over the high Alps and snow-passes, and down into Italy. On the outside of our carriage it said " *Venedig.*" It was the honeymoon train, but we were going another way. Yet, all the same, we were both gripped by excitement and awareness ; both of us felt that this was a journey into some unknown starlit mutual adventure. Frost brightened the air we breathed into our bodies that stood rocking in the hot stuffy corridor of the train. In time we came to snow-hills, and the smell of snow, and Glyndwr's narrow Welsh eyes sharpened, staring out across the cold peace of Semmering. We looked from the mountains to one another, talking in whispers, as behind us, in the darkened carriages, men and women settled uneasily to sleep. We talked about our lives and friends, and about politics, and about mountains, and, by and bye, we went back into our lightless carriage, and doubled coats to soften the wooden seats. At the far end, a father and son were asleep, their heads on their folded arms rested on the table-flap ; in front of us, a woman slept among bundles. We slept as best we could—our heads leaning and slipping ; our arms round each other ; our minds still full of the day's work. Even with a comrade, a night-journey third is tiring ; at my age one isn't supple enough for the narrow wooden seats. We woke at Bruck, our shut windows streaming with damp, and it seemed for a little as though it was rain. Somewhere, within a short way of the stopped train, our fellow Socialists were imprisoned ; we were terribly aware into what country we had come. It seemed to us, huddled

there, as though the sky, the world, were weeping
for Wallisch. But, when we came to Leoben and
the dark empty station, we saw that after all it
was a clear night.

We walked across the bridge, hearing below us the
quick muttering water that we knew must be
swollen with melted snow ; we were stiff and cold
and heavy. A railway-man showed us our way to
the main square and the hotel. We rang, and a
pleasant-faced youngish woman took us up. There
were apparently no single rooms, and we were too
tired to argue and explain, so we acquiesced in a
very large and magnificent double room, with pots
full of foliage plants, and windows looking out on to
the market-place. It was all extraordinarily cheap,
and they were nice people.

We were both too tired to say more than " Good
night " ; each of us curled under its fat red eiderdown,
hoping to flop asleep. But the morning's adrenalin
in my blood-stream had got to work, I suppose, on
thyroid and pituitary, and had set the vagus nerve
tugging at my heart, squeezing it like a tight hand
whenever I seemed at last to be relapsing into darkness. Outside, a clock kept on striking the quarters.
Glyndwr tossed about too, worrying over his report.
By and bye he asked for aspirin ; we each took two,
and, towards morning, both fell into nightmarish sleep,
from which we woke as the maid knocked and began
a rather unintelligible conversation which I inter-
preted as someone wanting Glyndwr on the telephone.

Glyndwr, incredibly blear-eyed, in a dressing-gown and rather gaudy pyjamas, staggered into the café, to hear someone telling someone else at the end of the telephone that he wasn't there. With great presence of mind he said he was—and duly telephoned to the Distinguished Belgian Colleague. The man at our end of the telephone was certainly the Person whom we had been told we might (or again conceivably might not) find in Leoben. He said to Glyndwr : " Are you an English M.P. ? " " No," said Glyndwr ; " are you ? " The other : " Well, really I have an American passport, but I call myself an English M.P. because they like it better." " Oh, all right," said Glyndwr ; " then I shall be a judge of the American High Court." In this slightly Balkan atmosphere they parted. Glyndwr reported to me, and said he was going to have a bath—he hadn't had time for one since he arrived in Austria, and he was feeling a bit fierce about it.

I heaved myself slowly into my clothes, and, while I was brushing my hair, a knock came at the door, and a head looked round : " Mr. —— ? " Seeing me, it was about to disappear, but I said firmly, " Come in. Mr. —— is in his bath. I'm Mrs. Mitchison." It appeared to me to be much too complicated to explain why I was there ; I had merely to trust to my actual, plain, matronly respectability. So I pinned up my hair with complete calm while a charming and soft-voiced Person in a crumpled blue shirt (whom I shall call Mr. Q.) explained that

226

he was now going to do so-and-so and so-and-so, and would come back for us after breakfast. I don't think he was really bothered ; he hasn't got that sort of silly mind.

In the bright, early sunlight we leaned out of the window to look at the market-square of Leoben, that Protestant and atheist town, all gay with fruit and vegetable stalls—bright piles of oranges and red cabbage and brown chestnuts—the little baroque cross, surrounded by gay, almost bouncing saints ; the fine house-fronts, showing off prosperities of two and three centuries back ; and beyond—forcing it all unalterably into character—a great shoulder of mountain, still streaked with late snow between the pines. At breakfast, Mr. Q. turned up again, and gave us various figures and facts. In this part of the world—that is to say, Austria south of Vienna —there are about 6,000 arrested. Re-arrests happen constantly ; he told us how people were taken from the court prisons to concentration camps—where the legal defence question is even more difficult. He told us how men who had been pronounced innocent by the court had been re-arrested by the police. Twenty or thirty had been loaded straight on to a lorry at the doors of the court, and taken off to the concentration camps.

We asked him about the political parties ; this is a part of the world where German Protestantism and German Nazi-ism are strong. But good Catholics, and also Nazis, are in some ways friendly with the

Social Democrats, making common cause against Fey and Starhemberg. He told us much else, which cannot at present be written down. And indeed, during the next two days, I saw and heard much which I cannot write here, which I had better forget if I can. Socialism is not dead in Austria, nor will it die.

We then went to see Mr. O., and Glyndwr discussed with him and his colleagues the question of legal defence. Whatever Mr. O.'s political views may be, he is that very startling thing, a real Christian. He has also persuaded some of his colleagues, and is struggling with the formidable business of legal defence for all the Socialist prisoners in this area. If he can defend them by working himself to death, no doubt he will. He is an oldish man and ill; he was gassed during the war—the *Welt-Krieg*, as we have to call it, to distinguish it from our own war of a month ago—perhaps by English chlorine. That just seems incredibly, uselessly, stupid now. His daughter was waiting to drive us to Graz ; we climbed into the back of a very smart and comfortable car, gloriously unlike a railway third, and the daughter from the driver's seat, leaned round and talked to us, sometimes petting a ridiculous little dog she had with her. She was plump and pretty, with a crop of curly black hair, a beret very much on one side, and a voice that cooed over her father. As he came out to join us, he was stopped in the street by a poor woman. "He would give the coat off his back!" said the girl, looking at him between smiles and tears. She asked us who we were, and we named ourselves, from America, Wales, and Scotland—a real international. "Gott sei dank," she said, "es gibt gute Leute!" And her voice cooed over us too. With both of them, one felt in the company of real goodness, and a kind of gaiety besides—which really good people (I am tempted to say, but *not* professional relief workers) somehow give out.

She drove splendidly and easily; it was raining, so we didn't see much. We talked and rested ourselves. Then we got to Graz, where our Distinguished Colleague had temporarily disappeared. We heard afterwards how, with a deliciously Gallic appropriateness, he had missed his way, gone into a house to telephone, been most kindly received, and, after the telephoning, asked to come down to the "dancing," which would be certain to give him every satisfaction! I gather he declined. We all forgathered at someone's flat, where a legal conference was held. By this time I was extremely sleepy, and did not understand much of what was happening, but Glyndwr nobly kept awake, and tells me that here again the legal position is bad; there are not enough lawyers willing to defend the prisoners; and there is no money. Some is expected from various sources, but much more will have to come if all the prisoners are going to come on trial.

In the meantime I had tried to telephone to

A. W., but she told me that she was expecting Frau Dollfuss and couldn't see me. We were to meet, instead, in Vienna. I had better say at once that Frau Dollfuss came, was very friendly and sensible, and quite agreed that her fund and our fund should work with some degree of collaboration, but, in general, separately. If Frau Dollfuss herself were really in charge, there would be no difficulty, nor do I think her colleague, Cardinal Innitzer, would disagree with her. Everyone could combine to pick up the bits. Unfortunately they are not the only ones who are running the fund ; Frau Dollfuss can no more stand up to the determined pressure of the Government than, say, the judicial system can. And this pressure is being brought to bear. Anyone in their senses—including even diplomats—can see that.

However, that was not yet clear when we left Graz. I had a talk to a visitor whose husband had been badly wounded, and lost a foot in the prison hospital, where one doctor had to look after an impossibly large number of wounded men. She was very anxious about him. Then I changed some money—which led Glyndwr to suppose that he wanted a hat (our accounts were by now hopelessly mixed). We went into a hat shop, and he tried on some lovely green hats, full of edelweiss and chamois feathers and goodness knows what-all ; they were very nice hats, *in vacuo*, but, when it came to the question of whether he would be able to wear them in The Temple, we reluctantly decided against them. There was only one hat he really liked, but, while he was trying it on, its owner came and politely reclaimed it. The next day, he bought some post-cards in Leoben instead ; after all, one can always send post-cards away !

We did well over our train, which at the cost of a tea each—which we needed—took us, with our third tickets, in the *wagon-restaurant*. We noticed, for the first time, the remark about getting drinks in the *wagon-lit*, and giggled helplessly over it, which shows the state of tiredness we were in, for it isn't perhaps really very funny—however, I commend it to anyone travelling. I explained that I felt like a Chinese egg—not very fresh—and he responded, dismally, that he felt like a Welsh rabbit. And so we came back to our hotel and the grand foliage of plants, and I had the inspiring thought that I, too, would have a bath.

However, we had a job to do first. And, after dusk, we set out to do it. The streets of Leoben were crowded with an apparently cheerful and light-hearted crowd, yet, as we went by, we kept on hearing the words we knew—" *Rechtsanwalt* " ; " *Ver-handlung* "—and, again and again, that word that comes so clear in a whisper—" *verhaftet* ; *verhaftet* " —arrested. Perhaps our ears were quick for those words, perhaps our very tiredness had keyed us up to a sharpening of all the senses engaged on our purpose.

Thus, we went through dark streets and past un-lighted houses, and, after a time, came to the place we needed, and, having established ourselves, were let in. There was a man, a woman, and a child. I said what we had come for. Slowly, with pauses while I looked up words in the dictionary, with pauses while I took notes, with pauses while the woman made us tea, or went to the door to make sure that we had not been followed, he told us the story of the last hours of Koloman Wallisch.

On the Sunday after the fighting—on the Sunday afternoon—it was known in Leoben, in the streets and the houses, and, at last, in the prison, that Koloman Wallisch was taken.

The story of Wallisch's life is another thing. He started as a plain worker, and he was never apart from the workers. He was an organiser and speaker, and an able and efficient man ; he had been through the Hungarian revolution and counter-revolution, and had seen his work destroyed. He had built it up again, with patience and thoroughness and gentleness. He was a kind and wise and humorous man. He was a party worker, and where the party sent him, he had to go, but when, last September, he was sent to organise from the small district of Bruck an der Mur to the great town and district of Graz, he told them in Bruck that if ever they needed him he would come back. At the beginning of the fighting the leaders at Bruck were arrested, and the metal workers and miners were disorganised, with no one to get them together and lead the Schutz-bund. They needed Wallisch, and Wallisch came. I do not know for certain how he was betrayed, nor the name of his betrayer. These betrayals are a black business, an after-taste of centuries of oppression. All I know is that someone did it.

The man said : " Wallisch was our God," and he laid his hands over his heart. He said : " It will be hard for me telling this." And the woman quivered and stared at us, and the child sat very still. In the pauses between his sentences everything was very still in that room, except the clock ticking on and over for three hours.

They brought Wallisch in a car to Leoben prison, and his wife with him. Sixty police came as his guard. To make doubly sure, and to make it worse for him and for all his friends, he was tied into the car with ropes, and had a grey cap jammed on to his head. The prison was overcrowded, and he was put into what used to be the women's part—into Cell 6. It is five paces long, and about six feet across. He was alone there, without friends, but they kept the door open the whole time. The police, in their steel helmets, stood all the time on guard by the door of the cell ; there were two police officers outside the window, and two inside the cell with Wallisch, watching him.

He stayed there until 2 p.m. on Monday, the next day, when the trial was to take place. The first two advocates whom he had asked for to defend him

were themselves already in prison ; another was ill.
One was selected for him by the court—Dr. Helmut
Wagner, a Socialist. The President of the Court was
Oberlandesgerichtrat Dr. Fritz Marinitsch, a man
who belonged to no political party. The prosecuting
counsel was Staatsanwalt Dr. Paul Suppan. Besides
Wallisch himself, there was one other man being
tried, a young official from Bruck. Wallisch was
forty-five years old.

In the centre of the prison there is a courtyard,
with wooden palings against the walls. It is called
the Holz Hof. On the day of the trial, before the
trial was begun, they set up the gallows there. It is
usual for some firm to tender for this work, but there
was no firm in Leoben which would touch it. The
criminals in the gaol were forced to build the gallows
that Monday morning. It was a wooden post, three
metres ninety in height, with a wooden bar at the
top, and four steps up to it. It was in the middle of
the Holz Hof. All round the Holz Hof were the cells
of the Socialist prisoners. They heard the gallows
being put up, and saw it there all that day.

On the Monday morning the hangman came from
Vienna. He was not the head-executioner of the
State, but a substitute, and his name was Spitzer.
With him came his two assistants. He went to the
largest hotel in Leoben, but, when they found out
there who he was, they turned him out. He went to
the café of the Hotel Post ; when they knew him,
they turned him out too. Then he went to a little

hotel, where, at first, they did not know who he was, and he and his assistants ordered schnapps and got drunk on it. When it had gone to their heads, they swaggered out in front of the other guests in the little hotel, and shouted what they were going to do. They scrawled a picture of the gallows. Then the hotel turned them out. All that Monday they went from place to place, first drunken and laughing, and then sobering down; wherever they went, every man and woman walked out. No one would take them in, and it began to be evening and the trial was still going on.

At 7 p.m., Dollfuss rang up, from Vienna; he himself spoke to the President of the Court, to ask why the trial was taking so long. He pressed the President to hurry it on. But it was 9.30 before it was over, and the death sentence was passed.

Those who are sentenced to death in Austria may plead for mercy to the Bundes President. Wallisch had said he would not ask for mercy, but his counsel, Dr. Wagner, thought it his duty to telephone to Vienna to the Ministry of Justice and lay the plea before them. He did this as soon as the trial was over, and Wallisch was taken back to Cell 6.

In the meantime everything had been made ready in the Holz Hof. It was floodlighted as bright as day, and at ten o'clock sixty soldiers marched in, with their officers. There were high officers from the army and high officers from the police, and the civil witnesses. And the prisoners were watching from their barred cells all round. Spitzer and his assistants were already there, seeing that all was right with their gallows.

Now, the man who was telling this, had seen it all from his cell, but what he told next was told him immediately afterwards by one of the police who were watching Wallisch. He was still speaking slowly, sweating a little, watching to see whether I had it right. He kept the story clear in the order of its happening. The little boy sat beside him, with his hands tight clasped between his knees. My pencil bluntened, and Glyndwr gave me another. As the story went on, I translated to him, and sometimes he would say something, but mostly he was silent, and again, sometimes a queer horrible laughter would shake both him and the man who was telling it.

In Cell 6, they asked Wallisch what were his last wishes, and he said he must speak with his wife Paula. These two had been in love with one another during their marriage ; she had lived only for him. She was a plump, gay woman, who liked running about, doing things for him and helping him ; who liked talking with neighbours and the life of a Socialist woman in a Socialist town. Now she was brought to the cell, but when she saw the police standing there she began to scream at them : " Mörder ! Henker ! "—Murderers ! Hangmen ! She screamed and screamed in the cell, but at last Wallisch quieted her. Then came her brother, and he was crying, and Paula was crying. Only Wallisch was not crying then.

There was a straw mattress in the cell, where he had lain on Sunday night, and now he and Paula sat on it, and he had an arm round her and stroked her head. She had brown bobbed hair. And still she went on crying, and at last Wallisch gave her a little smack on the knee, and said, laughing : " But I don't know whether it's you or me who is going to be hanged ! " And then, still laughing a little, he asked for all the newspapers they had, to know what was being said about him, and they brought them in, and he read them, and he laughed more.

And then again he asked for something. He asked for wine and a sweet tart, and they brought that. He had never before in his life drunk wine, but now he drank it almost all, leaving only a little. And the third hour came, and Paula knew, and began to scream.

As the man said that, the child began to cry too, quietly and dreadfully. He was quite white. The man kissed him, and I said good night, and the woman took him away to bed. Then the story went on.

The prison doctor came, with a handkerchief soaked in chloroform, and Wallisch put one arm round Paula and the other hand, with the handkerchief, up against her face. He chloroformed her, and laid her down on the straw mattress in the cell.

And then he said that he had yet one more wish.

He asked them to bring in to him three comrades from Bruck, who had fought beside him, and who were now prisoners. He needed to speak with them once more. So that, too, was done. They brought in the three comrades. He said : " Bleibt weiter aufrechte Proleten. Es wird wieder der Tag kommen an dem wir siegen werden. Das Schwerste wird mit meinem Tod vorüber sein. Man wird nach mir keinen mehr hängen und das Standgericht aufheben." This is, in English : " You must stay true proletarians. The day will yet come for which we were fighting. When I am dead the worst will be over. After me there will be no more hanging, and the courts martial will be finished." And then he shook hands with each of them, and they were taken back. And it was now a little after 11.30.

The call came through from Vienna, from the Ministry of Justice, to say that they would not lay Wallisch's appeal before the Bundes President. This news was brought to the cell by Dr. Marinitsch and the two counsel. He said : " I knew." And thanked them for their fair trial.

There was a reason for this thanks. Wallisch was speaking in his own defence, and, after half an hour, the President had asked him if this was a time for oratory, and he had answered : " Herr President, remember that this is the last time in my life that I shall make a speech." And the President said, " You are right. Go on." You must know that Wallisch had always been a speaker who could grip his

audience, not a great classical orator, but he always
went to the point, and he could make people laugh
or cry with him. And now he spoke as he had never
spoken before. Most of that speech is known now to
the workers of Leoben and Bruck ; it goes from hand
to hand, hidden under a book or in a tea-pot, then
coming out again, and passing on. But, while he was
speaking it, the prosecuting counsel wanted to stop
him ; he interrupted. Wallisch turned on him, and
said, " Be quiet. This is on my head, not yours."
And the President of the court said he was to go on.
So this was why he thanked them now, in truth, for
their fairness.

Then Spitzer came into the cell, and he said,
" Come on out." But Wallisch said to him quietly,
" You must still wait a moment." Then they asked
him if he wanted to see a priest, but he refused that
firmly and, some say, laughing again a little. He
stood there in his blue worker's clothes, and then
suddenly the two assistants got him, one on each
side, and hurried him, frog-marched, down the long
prison passage into the Holz Hof.

And now all the prisoners, fifty or sixty of them,
were hanging by their hands on to the bars of their
cells, to see their Wallisch just once again. The man
who was telling this, and whose eyes were now
blinking with tears, watched him go by the window—
with his head held high, as though he were at a great
political meeting. He went past as proud and gay and
brave as he had always been. Only, when he came

239

to the corner and saw the floodlit gallows, he checked for a moment, only a second, and then went on between his executioners.

The soldiers were all round the court. It was thought that something might happen—they did not quite know what—something that they did not want anyone outside to hear. But it was not necessary. There was no screaming now.

He stood at the post, with his back against it. Spitzer, the hangman, went up the steps, with his white gloves and his black hat ; he tied the end of the rope over the cross-piece ; he put the noose round Wallisch's neck. And then Wallisch shouted : " Es lebe die Sozial Demokratie, hoch ! Freiheit ! " But the last syllable of the last word—*Freiheit*—was choked out of him.

Spitzer, from above, gripped and tightened the rope, and the two below pulled him down, clinging on to his legs, and then on to his shoulders, strangling him down, one at each side, pulling him dead. But after he lost consciousness, after the struggling ceased and the hangmen let go, it was still twelve minutes before he died. For he was a strong man. Two doctors were feeling the pulse at his wrist, and, when it was quite finished, Spitzer came down the steps. He took off his white gloves and threw them away ; he went to the President of the court, took off his bowler hat, and said : " Ich melde das Urteil ist vollstreckt," which is in English, " I notify you that sentence has been carried out."

And then, at last, the judge and the counsel went away, and the civil witnesses, and, last of all, the soldiers. But the fifty or sixty Socialist prisoners were watching still, and, as the gentlemen went by them, one of the prisoners shouted " Murderers ! " against them.

Now, the man who was telling me this had been amongst those prisoners, and told me how the police came quickly to the cells and searched for the man who had shouted that. But there was no one to betray him, and he was never found. I asked then, " Were the prisoners ill-treated or beaten to make them tell ? " but he said, " No, there was no ill-treatment. If I had said there was, that would have been *Greuel-Lüge* (atrocity propaganda). You must have only the truth about Wallisch."

So the soldiers marched away out of the Holz Hof, but the floodlights were left turned on to the gallows, and for two hours the body of Wallisch hung there, alone, and for two hours his comrades at the bars of their cells watched over it. But at the end of the two hours, at 1.30 in the dark morning of February the 20th, they heard the jangle and grating of keys in the door of the Holz Hof. Spitzer and the two, and six soldiers, came over to the gallows and took down the body, and laid it into a black shroud. They took it away, and into a car, which was waiting outside the prison ; the prisoners heard it starting and the gears changing, and heard it drive away into the night.

There had been no workers allowed at Wallisch's

trial. Admission cards had only been given to good Catholics of safe families. Most of the lookers-on were ladies—if that is the way to speak of them. For the workers there was another kind of looking-on. They had been up all night, waiting. They were hiding in corners of the streets and on the hill-side. The moon was in its first quarter, and would scarcely have given any light, but they were watching with binoculars, and followed the car on its way to the cemetery, which lies by the river, a little outside of Leoben. Spitzer and the soldiers took the body, out of the car, into the cemetery ; they locked the door of the cemetery, for they were afraid that they might be followed. But there were men climbing and peering over the walls, and a few of these comrades saw and marked the place. The body of Wallisch was hidden in behind another grave-stone, and the earth flattened over it, as a dog might be buried. And the soldiers and the hangmen left it there, and went back quickly, and thought that no one would know.

But in the morning that flattened grave was a heap of flowers ; some were evergreens, and some were snowdrops and Christmas-roses ; some were made like Schutzbund badges, and some like the Three Arrows. Later in the morning the police were told, and came, and took away the flowers. But it was the same the next night, and again the police took the workers' flowers, and threw them into the road. For three days they did this, and then a letter came to the overseer of the cemetery, who is a Heimwehr man, and the letter said : " If you take away our flowers, you yourself will be taken away." And the priests were afraid, and advised that the flowers should be left. So now there are flowers there always, fresh and fresh every day.

On Easter Saturday (which is less than a fortnight from the day I am writing, but which will be over before this is in print) the good Catholics go to their *Heilige Grab*, to the service of watching by the painted wooden bodies of their Leader. In this country, six soldiers stand in the churches by the Body of Christ. But on the same day, thousands and thousands of workers from Leoben and Bruck and Graz, from Vienna and Linz and St. Pölten and Innsbruck, and all over Upper and Lower Austria, will come to their *Heilige Grab* in the little cemetery of Leoben. Word has gone to them, and is going, from hand to hand and mouth to mouth. In the early morning, one worker will climb into a tree with the Red flag, and make it fast there—he will be arrested, but that does not matter. And all day there will be six workers, in their blue workers' clothes, watching by the body of their Leader, as the soldiers watch in the churches. And as every six are arrested and taken away, so another six will be ready to come.

So it came to the end of the story, and we stood up to go. I think we had all been weeping a little. In another room the little boy lay asleep. Outside it was late and dark. Glyndwr and I went back, speaking in whispers, breathing uneasily. We came to our hotel, and ate together, knowing that we were both in some way changed by this. We were both deadly tired, yet it was hard to sleep. I think we were both afraid. I know that I was afraid, for it seemed to me that there was a burden laid upon me to write about Koloman Wallisch, and I did not know for sure whether I could do it. Only I was glad at least that I was a good craftsman, and I was very glad now to be with a comrade. We were both glad of that.

Perhaps most men and women, in these circumstances, might have wanted to make love to one another ; but we were in the grip of something older, and yet younger—something more powerful and less individual than that. It seemed as though our deepest and fiercest emotions were at bursting-point, and yet all momently fused into the clarity of this fact that we were *Genossen*—comrades. We were lost together, there in the dark room, holding one another by the hand, talking sometimes and sometimes quiet, only that Glyndwr would break the quiet, muttering horribly to himself : " *Verhaftet ; verhaftet* . . ." But, after a time, even that stopped, the worst things began not to hurt, we dropped into thick sleep.

Early the next morning we had our flowers— flowering heather, and red carnations and hyacinths. I had written a card, which said, in our bad German ; " An Wallisch, Helden den ganzen Welt, von

Englischen Arbeitspartei Genossen. Mit Liebe." And
then I had written the names of the places I thought
that Glyndwr and I could stand for : " London,
South Wales, Oxford, Cambridge, King's Norton,
Salford, Glasgow." And I had added : " Und auch
von Belgischen Genossen." For the Distinguished
Colleague had asked us to do that for him.

It was a most lovely day, full of softness and bright
sweet colours—the sky, the mountains, the river,
the wide square and narrow streets of Leoben,
half in sun and half in chilling shadow. As we went
by, it became known that here were two English
Genossen, they, too, bringing flowers to the Holy
Grave. In the open streets there were smiles and
hand-clasps, and, over and over again, the scarcely
whispered *Freundschaft*. After Vienna, I was nervous
and delighted. And so we came, at last, to the grave-
yard, and our companion led us, openly and without
haste, towards the grave of Wallisch.

When this was dug, on Monday the 19th of
February, not quite a month before, another grave-
pit was made too, for the young official who was
tried with Wallisch. But the official was pardoned,
and is in prison, and the grave was filled in, so that
we stood on or beside it, looking down at the other.
It was one great mass of flowers—pine and spruce
branches, and silver or pale gold pussy-willow, and
fresh Christmas-roses, and violets and mimosa, and
some paper flowers. Only, there was nothing written.
Every two hours a policeman comes and takes away

cards and inscriptions—as they took away the one
that was put there the third day after the entomb-
ment, which said, "To our unforgotten Leader.
The last greetings from Bruck." There were a few
bees on the pussy-willow ; it looked like the grave of
someone much loved just after mourners had left
it, but it has been like this all the time. Ever since.

A couple of women came and stood by us, then
a man. Then another man. Before we had been
there ten minutes, there were ten or fifteen other
comrades there with us, mostly men, but a few
women. There was one man in a green-faced
peasant's coat and green hat, come from St. Peter,
over the mountains. Speaking in a difficult dialect,
he told us of his two imprisoned sons, one of whom,
a seventeen-year-old, had been badly beaten when
he was captured. Here, by the grave, he could
speak of all that. Another man from up the valley
came, and asked, in a whisper, if this were really the
Grave. He had not made the pilgrimage before. They
talked about Wallisch—how he was *unvergesslich* ;
how there was no forgetting such a man. They talked
of the trial and the death. And someone said, with
tears in his eyes, thinking of Wallisch's companions :
"One must be ashamed to walk in the sun, when
there are still in the prisons the best of the good."
And again, two men whispering together, and one
saying that this was the "*neue Christus-Leben.*" There
were many tears there, strong faces, blurred and
twitching with tears. I thought I had seen these

faces and these tears before, and remembered
Breughel. I was remote enough to do that, to think
of a picture, and yet we were partly with them, we
wanted to be ; we too could share it—*Juxta crucem
tecum stare*. And then, after a time, it seemed to me
that the weeping faces hardened and brightened—
that something had come to them. After ten or
twenty minutes they can go, healed and strengthened,
as a Christian is healed and strengthened by prayer
at some other holy place.

As we left, we passed two other pilgrims, an old
woman, weeping, held up by a younger one. This
is a place where things can be said and promised
and believed, and where Socialists can be sure that
nothing has been in vain. And again, on our way
back to Leoben, there were others coming, some
with bunches of flowers ; they came on foot or on
bicycles, bringing string-bags, with bread and
sausage to eat. More come on Saturdays and
Sundays. It appeared to be known that we had been
there ; they smiled and nodded at us. One old
woman, with a black silk handkerchief over her
head, told us she went every morning early to tidy
the grave ; they had threatened to imprison her for
that. " I have never been in prison my whole life,"
she said, " and I am an old woman now. But I
would do that for Wallisch."

A little further down the street, we came to the
prison. Five or six Socialist prisoners were coming
down the street, carrying their bedding and bundles ;

they were being taken from one of the temporary
emergency prisons to the main prison, which is
now not so full as it was. They were grinning and
swaggering, waving at friends in the street, and
behind them marched a solitary policeman with a
rifle, looking rather out of it. However, when he
saw us all smiling, he had, at last, to smile himself.

There was now a certain amount of conversation,
exceedingly interesting as showing what is happening
in the minds of people in Central Europe, and, at the
end of the conversations, we were told we might see
Frau Wallisch. We waited in a wide stone passage,
with pot-plants in it, which had once been a cloister.
And, after a time, a door opened, and we saw a
woman in a fur-bordered coat, with a lank, untidy
bob of hair, coming slowly towards us, walking
very lame, and shaking from head to foot. But it
was her face that I think I shall never forget. There
are faces like it in Breughel's " Massacre of the
Innocents," or his woman who is set upon by thieves ;
there are faces like it in German crucifixion pictures
—the faces of the Marys at the foot of the cross.
They did not stop me going to her, and putting
my arms round her, and leading her so across the
cloister to a bench. It must, I think, have been
fairly obvious what kind of things I was whispering
to her, but theoretically they were unheard. I do
not know how much she understood herself, but I
think she must have known that they were friendly

248

arms round her neck, a friendly cheek against her
wet cheek, hands stroking her hair—as his had done.
And she sobbed, saying quiveringly that it was all
right for her, but there were others, poorer, with
little children—what was being done for them?
And then she said, dreadfully : " If only I could
see him once again," and her voice thickened and
broke into tears. It did not seem to me that anyone
in that prison wanted to keep Paula Wallisch shut
in a cell. They were decent people. They would
not let me take her back all the way, but they
spoke to her and helped her very kindly. It remains
to be seen what the Government will do with
her.

We walked to the station after that, but found
we had missed our train, so decided to walk, at any
rate half-way to Bruck. Glyndwr had got into a
curious habit of calling me *Gnädige Frau*—gracious
lady. I thought he did it to laugh at me for not
being a real proletarian as he is, and I wished he
would call me *Genossin*, but thought I mustn't
mind being teased. However, he really did it because he thought it was a term of endearment !
But it made the other comrades laugh—one of them,
saying good-bye, called me *Gnädige Frau*, and
pinched my chin, and smiled with a capital friendli-
ness. We talked to many there, and heard enough
of what was happening. There was bad enough
economic distress in Leoben and Donauwitz, and
round about, before all this : now it is ten times

worse, but very hard to say just how much any given piece of distress is caused by the earlier or the later conditions.

It was wonderfully warm by mid-morning ; I put coat and cap into my rucksack, and walked bare-armed in a shirt. We thought we must go and see the grave once more, and went back. There was a man standing there ; he told us the police had taken our card already, but we should write another and lay it deeper among the flowers. We did that. Since the early morning, when we had been first, there were more flowers—a pot of flowering cinerarias, and many little bunches. Now, too, in the warm mid-morning, there were bees everywhere on the flowers, coming and going busily through the sweet air. They were the first bees I have seen this year, and I saw none on any of the other graves which had flowers on them.

Our road followed the course of the river, which was very full, grey-green with melted snow water, hurrying down, foaming a little. Above it, on our right, were the small hills, and streaks of snow coming down very nearly to our level. Above and beyond them, the great snow mountains. It would have been lovely to climb up there into the snow, and have all this frozen and cleaned out of us in the bright cool whiteness. But we had to stick to the road, where already the earliest flowers were beginning to show, the ragged gay coltsfoot, gutter-child of March, and sometimes a daisy.

But it was a grand walk, even on the road ; it was my first real let-up since I've been here, and I thought I deserved it. I felt fantastically happy. Glyndwr told me I must take care not to use " *Genossen* as journalism." I knew what he meant, and I know it's my danger, and I know I've got to be warned about it from time to time. All along the road there were men in their green-striped trousers, coats with green facings and horn buttons, embroidered waistcoats, and these delightful hats full of trophies, and women in aprons and shawls. If the Wallisch hero-cult has brought in the peasants too, it will have done more than Marx ever did. I don't know if these people were peasants or workers —miners, for instance—in their best clothes. At least their faces were not like the faces in Vienna.

In one place there was a great swastika cut in the turf of the hill-side, and, in the anti-Nazi Government posters, the Nazi symbol on the villain and his big stick had been scratched out. That is certainly the alternative. I don't suppose there are more than a hundred Communists in the whole district.

We had *Mittagessen* and good cider in a wayside pub—good food ; peasants' food. And then the Bruck train came in, so crowded that we could only just squeeze into the corridor. At Bruck station there were quantities of young men and particularly jolly looking girls in trousers and bright coloured caps— all with skis and ski-sticks—climbing into the train, and laughing and shouting. I wondered how many of them were Nazis. It would have been fun to be going with them !

Bruck an der Mur is a lovely little town, with an even more beautiful and welcoming market-square than Leoben. Here we bought photographs, from two shops, both very sympathetic. They had photographs of the war—Schutzbund and Heimwehr in action ; and photographs, too, of the dead, including Linhart, who had bled to death during two days, with doctors and friends kept from him at the bayonet-point. One shop had photographs of Wallisch, better than any newspaper ones I had seen ; it is difficult not to look at this photograph without its content of history. I took three, and the man in the shop put down another handful on to the table, and asked me if I had yet seen the Grave. That is the sort of place Bruck is.

I tried to find a comrade there, while Glyndwr went off to do his legal business. My woman was not to be found, so I wandered back to the café, on the way buying five little silver buttons for Lois—my one extravagance so far ! I wrote letters, and by and bye Glyndwr turned up, complete with a charming and sympathetic judge, and a young friend of his, a German mathematician, with whom I had various mutual academic acquaintances. It seemed all very odd, being polite and theoretical again, and into one's usual pleasant, ironic, rather tired atmosphere. Glyndwr had been taken over the famous Bruck prison with the machine gun on the stage pointing at the prisoners, but conditions were much better there than they were even a short time ago. After all, one gets used to a machine gun. Aren't we all living with the equivalent of that pointing at us! The prison was much less overcrowded, and the prisoners sounded as though they were having not too bad a time—except, of course, that they didn't know what was going to happen to them. And the fact that, as the judge explained to us, they were getting better food inside the prison than they ever would have outside it, did not point to a very satisfactory home-coming. Most of them would lose their jobs. Some of them came up to the judge, Glyndwr said, begging for news of release, or even of trial, but he could give them no hope.

This was not very cheering, especially when we heard also the many stories of re-arrest. We saw a few prisoners being marched through the streets here. And, again, we are constantly hearing " war-stories " from the early times. One lawyer told us of a man he had defended early on, who had been accused of shooting a policeman. The funeral was arranged to coincide with the time of hearing, and, as it went past, Heimwhr men rushed in, clamouring at the judge to condemn the accused man. But the judge stood up to them, and got the lawyer and his client both out of the court before they were lynched. I get the feeling that justice will be done unless the Government puts impossible pressure to bear on the judiciary, or so alters the proceedings that its own sentences will be given. Any International Legal Commission which may be set up must not interfere with the judges, but must instead stand between them and their own Government.

From Bruck, again, we came back in the *wagon-restaurant*, eating their expensive and dull dinner, but saving ourselves aches and pains. Next us was a man also eating the dinner—but with hock and coffee and pears, and all possible extras—opposite a blonde and sparkling lady, who was entertaining him beautifully. He was a stupid-looking man, but she was inclining to fat. I kept on thinking how odd it must be to be someone's mistress and to acquire the sense—which she obviously had—that she'd got not only the right, but a kind of duty, to possess quantities of things, the more expensive the better.

We took a taxi from the station, feeling rather gay and triumphant. Glyndwr had done his legal work magnificently—much better, as it turned out, than any of the others ; and I had something, which was at the very least epic, to get my teeth into. We felt we deserved rather well of the world. We took a taxi to Sam's, and put on our rucksacks again, so as to be able to swagger in and be, as it were, re-turned warriors. But no luck—everyone was out. So back to the hotel, to swagger, if possible, over Evert ! But there we found two letters waiting for us from home, with a scolding for Glyndwr for having taken too much upon himself. He didn't say much, but he got very red in the face, and I thought he was going to cry. I was pretty cross myself : it seemed so like home conditions, and the way people can't realise that things can't just be left over here—one's got to take responsibilities and act quickly and on one's own initiative. They ought to have been grateful to him as a comrade, instead of saying he ought to have waited—until, no doubt, a committee had met and considered the matter for a week, and then sent out an official letter ! Actually, as we found out later, it wasn't really so much people at home, as a misunderstanding between there and here, due to the difficulties of telephoning across Europe and having everything overheard. But, being young, Glyndwr was badly hurt by it ; I wrote back to England, like an aunt, saying as firmly and tactfully as I could what we thought over here. There's no Sunday air-mail, so those bloody letters had to be taken all the way over to the West Bahnhof! In the middle, Evert turned up, just a little drunk perhaps. We didn't tell him this, but we told him our other adventures. When it came to the bedroom scene, he appeared rather perturbed. That sort of thing seems completely ludicrous, considering that Glyndwr and I have never so much as kissed one another. I made them both tea—but Glyndwr likes disgusting black proletarian tea with lots of milk and sugar, and I only make highbrow tea, pale and aromatic with lemon !

After all that, the next day didn't seem very

thrilling, but I had a fearful lot to do. A good deal
of the time was spent, as usual, waiting about, in
one place or another, for someone who was in fact
waiting for one somewhere else. There was plenty
of news—things never stay still here ! The money is
coming out very efficiently, and we feel now that
Transport House is great and good, that its wheels,
although they grind slowly, do grind exceeding
small, and so on. But the Quakers have the wind up,
and no wonder ! The Government are demanding
that they should turn over their lists of helpers to
the police, someone has been put in as a kind of
commissioner who is really not at all what is needed ;
the Dollfuss–Innitzer fund is pressing for closer
co-operation, in fact that they should run things
their own way ; the organisation is pretty bad, and
lots of people have had no help. Even the Legation
is as grieved as the official mind can be. Or perhaps
it isn't. I don't know. I can't understand legations ;
I find it easier to get into intimate contact with the
sea-lions at the Zoo ! However, that, no doubt, is
my fault. Several extremely worrying and rather
alarming things have happened, and they need
someone with some guts to put them right. Unfortunately, most of the guts in this country are on
the Social Democratic side—or possibly some are
to be found among the Nazis. But if I go into the
question of whether Mr. So-and-so or Miss Such-an-
one has any guts, and, if so, where, I should doubtless
be in for a libel action.

Apart from that, I had to write diary and a few letters. Such letters as had been forwarded from home were all annoying and silly, and appear to involve my being bothered as soon as I get back to London. Lunch in the hotel, with all the waiters listening in, as usual ; I amused myself with inventing some stories for their benefit, and telling them in a loud voice.

Mr. Q. and Mr. P. were both wanted, and both missing. Whenever any of the " Foreign Legion " met any of the others, they always asked if the two missing links had yet been found. A. W. came to dinner with Glyndwr and me, but I left her to him, for my head was full of the Wallisch story. I liked her, though ; she was handsome and capable, and full of fun and intelligence. If only one had time to make friends with all the people one would really like to know !

All that evening I wrote the story of Wallisch, keeping carefully to the notes I had made, and in the end it broke me completely and when Glyndwr came in, after one of his midnight café committee-meetings, I was crying over my typewriter. I read it to him, getting the poison out of myself into him, but that's all right between *Genossen*. Then he went off to his new room in a nice, comfortable flat. But so far he has been too shy to ask the owners where the w.c. is.

MARCH 19TH

Mostly diary to-day, and also periodical bumpings-up against, say, Comrades H. to L. And telephone calls, and arrangements to be made and unmade. It seems likely, on precedents, that I may be severely searched at the frontier, so Grace is making a pocket inside my knickers ! On coming out of Ian's flat, a woman stepped towards me, had a good look at me, and wrote something down in a note-book. I was nearly sick. Also a long wrangle with a reluctant Cook's office, from whom I finally extracted the money they had for me.

Again I am incredibly tired ; someone should have come to see me half an hour ago with certain information ; thank goodness she hasn't turned up, and now probably won't ! For some reason I can't sleep late in the mornings, even when I have the chance. I wish I could hear some music or see some pictures—painted ones, I mean, in a museum !—or even sit quite quietly in a café and think about nothing. But there isn't time. And to-morrow I have to meet someone at nine in the morning. I almost feel I deserve the embroidered jersey, but I can't see myself having time to go and buy it ! All the same, I should like to stay—I can't bear the idea of leaving all this reality—and I know when I go back I shall have to make speeches, which I hate, try to put all this across to inert people in England, already sufficiently occupied with their own problems. And I know I shall do it badly.

I got some quite interesting information about doctors this morning. The *Krankenkasse*, which is the Government sickness insurance scheme, has sent round *questionnaires* to all the doctors, asking them to give their nationality (and since when they have held it) and their religion (with the same question). There is any amount of anti-Semite propaganda, and also action, going on. The usual sexy anti-Semite lies about doctors and girl patients ; that's to be expected. I expect the priests get the hell of a kick out of it. Most hospitals are turning out their Jewish doctors, too. And, as in Germany, there is the old correlation between Jew and Marxist. There are moments when I devoutly wish that this were true !

Glyndwr has produced a letter from home, which has obviously been tampered with—and it was in Welsh ! I don't think any of us mind any of that for ourselves, but then we have the big blue passports. It's our friends who haven't that we need to worry about.

I've been washing my own stockings, and various oddments for the young men. It's curiously restful. I feel guilty about the state of my accounts, but one can't do everything, and higher mathematics (which is the way I regard these transactions between pounds and Schillings) was never my strong suit. I think I am beginning to blither. I think I have got a cold. I believe what I need is alcohol.

After dinner. The alcohol was only mildly effective —and I'm sure about the cold ! I've been going over the Wallisch report, which Glyndwr has written from my story. I want to rewrite several things, but don't know whether I'm being highbrow about it. Glyndwr, in the meantime, is talking to P. and Q. Also, having got fifty pounds from Dick, he has bought me a big bunch of snowdrops. Only, all flowers remind me now of Wallisch's grave.

MARCH 20TH

Trotting about all to-day. In the morning went to get a permit to visit the children's home, then to a Jewish organisation to try and find out what was happening to Jewish children. But I got nothing, only an impression of very competent Jewish women doctors. Then I got to G.'s, to find him with a young man from Canada, a thick-set, dark, young man, with a diplomatic visa. He had a nice typical " war-story," of how he had gone to be shaved at the barber's shop where Dollfuss goes, but, not finding his assistant, he had turned and gone away. Being the sort of the young man who runs down stairs, he *had* run downstairs, only to be stopped at the bottom by two plain-clothes men, with, " Whither away ? " He was kept in the police-station all day, examined and re-examined, and not allowed to communicate with the consulate. And all because this suspicious act of running downstairs had made them certain that he was about to assassinate the Chancellor, or possibly had left a bomb behind him !

The young man was a musician and ridiculously unpolitical—one felt quite angry with him for that. G. had been seeing prisons, and said they were still fearfully overcrowded. It was all very well for the big bugs in the separate cells with their books and newspapers and special food, but still bad for the others. I keep on hearing of desperately ill men being put into these big crowded cells with twenty or thirty others.

Then I came back, saw Mrs. T., M., and C., and discussed things. And then a half hour opened in front of me, and M. and C. and I all went off to the great museum to look at pictures. It was an extraordinary half hour. I don't think I've ever seen pictures with such delight and apparently such understanding before. They seemed exciting and new as they never have before. I began to wonder whether one ought ever to look at pictures without having done some hard work first. It seemed to me that perhaps one can't otherwise appreciate the *praxis* pictures—such as Breughel's figure paintings— or the calm and phantasy pictures like Jan Breughel's flowers or Van der Goes's delicious " Garden of Eden." It was all very odd. One could follow it out from the bland early fifteenth century, apparently an age of at least innocence, through the growing pain and confusion of the sixteenth, with Breughel painting every torture and misery, to the sudden civilisation of Holbein, who seems definitely not of our time—since we too are in the midst of dark ages and something too like religious wars—something we can admire but never understand.

Breughel was extraordinary after all I have seen. There is the face of the woman who is fighting the soldiers in the " Bearing of the Cross," and many faces in the " Massacre of the Innocents." All that desperation and horror and hideous, enforced submission—and the cruelty on the other faces. One could see, in the massacres, which were regular army and which were Heimwehr. Only there aren't any Schutzbund yet ; they were to come later. And all these centuries people have been horribly and irrevocably oppressed, and all Breughel could do was to paint them, and all I can do is to write about them, and, until they have ceased to submit, nothing else can be done. There was a baddish picture by Geertgen von Haarlem, a pieta, crudely painted, but the faces were pure Floridsdorf. And again and again one of the weeping and broken Marys brought back to me the face of Paula Wallisch, weeping those same helpless and dreadful tears.

I wonder why Dürer seems so much happier. And

yet he's full of it too. I was looking at his curious, untypical altar-piece. Here is the crucified victim, and all earth and heaven grouped round him. But the kings and popes are respectfully failing to understand in the least, and the queens are gossiping, and the saints are bored. There is one old man, with a fur cap, in a corner, who seems really rather moved, but none of the others is, including the impassive Father. And the Son of Man has been so beaten up, and generally put through it, that he simply can't explain any more.

After that I had lunch with Lass, stopping on the way to buy some spring flowers for her hostess. She tells me that all schoolboys have to wear the Vaterlandische Front badge—and according to which way it is worn, pointing right or left, and so on, one can tell whether a boy is Socialist, Communist, Nazi, or unpolitical ! I left her a little money, in case she found urgent need for it. She had seen the little schoolmaster, looking desperately ill and miserable ; all the people who were arrested with her have been released ; most of it was a silly police muddle, not a betrayal. I was glad of that.

From there back, and to look at a charming children's home, which keeps children, who are being sent to families or country homes, for a period of three weeks' quarantine before they are passed on. It is still being run much as it was, and is a grand building, with all the latest appliances, and three-quarters full of children. Every bit of it is in duplicate, so that, if there is infection, one side can be shut off. The children from three months to six are in groups of six, both sexes together, older ones are in groups of eighteen and do a certain amount of lessons. I was impressed with the general look of the place, efficient and at the same time beautiful, with very intelligent-looking nurses and students. There is a place for gymnastics, and a lovely garden for games. In old days, children who were cripples or mentally deficient—those least likely to be useful to the community—were sometimes sent to nunnery schools, but most of the others went to families or Socialist children's homes. But the latter have been closed by the Government, so more and more have to go to the nunnery schools. I wonder what it will all be like in another six months ?

Yesterday, Glyndwr and I had had a frantic time typing out a Wallisch article which we thought was to go into various foreign papers—however, it seems unlikely to be going to get further than Zurich ! I was a little fed up to see all our labour go for so little —and also the translation (which Sam had done), and the typing (which I had done) of Wallisch's last speech ! Mr. P. and Mr. Q. were unaware of how we had sweated. Still—— They had tea in my room, one taking it highbrow, the other lowbrow. Evert also turned up, and the evening ended in something like a free fight between Glyndwr and Evert.

Oh, and I forgot my shopping ! I suddenly decided I *would* get the embroidered jersey, whatever

happened, so I went to the shop—and then the jerseys
didn't seem so nice after all, at least not on me, so I
got a frock instead ! It's a printed linen peasant's
frock, and it's very pretty, and cost thirty-six
Schillings, which doesn't seem desperately much.
And I got some embroidered ribbon for Lois, and
some little silly things for the children, and two
lovely coloured wreaths to put round the necks of
wine bottles for Dick's birthday.

I had tea with Glyndwr, though rather hurriedly,
as we had to see G., and then I came home and typed
like hell to get something done in time for Janet to
take back to England. Then Anne turned up, and
we discussed things, trying to see how it would all
seem from England. It seems incredible that I
should be going back—I just can't quite imagine
what it'll be like. But I've got to be at a meeting an
hour after my train arrives on Sunday ! I know
when I get back I shall feel I've over-simplified ;
that I've left out international factors ; that it's not so
plain and simple as it looks from here—and I shan't
be able to explain all that to Anne because she'll be
here. I wish she were coming back with me.

Then I went to dinner with G.—the usual excellent
meal—and discussed things again, though more
ordinarily. Everything feels beautifully ordinary and
un-intense when G. has debunked it ! Afterwards
to see —— and ——. The situation seems to me to be
rather worrying.

MARCH 21ST

The day of the equinox—spring. I felt all day as if
I were making it happen. We started early, after some
running round changing money, and got a slow
train to Wiener Neustadt. Part of the time Glyndwr
and I stood on the rattling, bumping, windy platform
of the train, and I was exceedingly happy. So, I
think, was he. It seemed to me then how simple
and easily attainable the elements are that make up
human happiness, the thing which makes our years
of living valid. Bright sun, mountains in the distance,
and in the foreground scrubby fields of vine-stocks,
and here and there a willow coming into bud;
going somewhere on a job—the pause and gathering
up of the spirit before work starts ; the rush of air ;
above all the *Solidarität*, the comradeship. It seemed
to me that any civilisation which was worth the price
of its existence ought to be able to give us that. We
were travelling third, wearing oldish clothes ; we
had a couple of oranges, and a bit of chocolate—that
was all in the way of amenities. But it was spring
all right. I hope I shall die when I stop feeling the
spring.

Wiener Neustadt is pretty, a typical Austrian
country town, with old houses, pleasant bits of
ancient wall, empty and sunny spaces, much the
same now as they had been a hundred or two
hundred years ago. There was an old courtyard we

passed through, with high red roofs tilted to a gorgeous steepness, and there is a market-place, where to-day they were selling great heaps of glowing apples and blood oranges, and hundreds of little fruit-trees, foliage-bushes, and seedling vines. There were wicker-sided carts, which the vegetables had come in, and heaps of baskets and wooden farm things. We stopped at a little beer-house, and had execrable coffee and a delicious *Bretzel*. Then we set out to find our friends. My introduction was no use. I was told to go to the Arbeiterheim, but it was being occupied by Heimwehr, so I didn't pursue my enquiry ; I found out later that the man was in prison.

However, Glyndwr's introduction proved successful. The husband was in prison, but the wife could give us the information we needed. They had a charming little house with modern furniture and curtains—from which they are probably going to be turned out. He was doing rather well in his profession ; so was she ; now all that's over. The daughter had hoped to go to college. Now——

We gathered a pretty gloomy picture of the town. Everyone is frightened. Almost all the leaders were arrested before the Monday, so there was no fighting. At least five hundred are in prison, either in the court prison, or in an *Anhaltelager* : perhaps more. They have never had any charge against them, so they can't be defended, even if lawyers were found to undertake the defence. But there are none of them ; they are too frightened. And distress is bad. Three thousand men, about ten per cent of the population, were unemployed before, owing to the shutting of the munition factory and various big engineering firms ; it was bad enough for their families before. But now it's a hundred times as bad ! Nothing has been heard of the Government relief fund.

(While I was writing this, we had bad news. Someone has been arrested, and it is not known who will be implicated. I am waiting for Glyndwr to come back with any information he can get. There are certain things which I think ought to be done.)

To go on with Wiener Neustadt. We went round with the daughter of the house, to see various people who were out, and then had lunch ourselves— excellently, at the local restaurant, with a delicious and cheap quarter-litre of wine. Then we went off in opposite directions on our errands.

I went to see a very nice, capable woman who had been doing distribution of the Quaker money. The first week she had given six Schillings all round —not much for families who had sometimes been three weeks without a wage-earner. The second week she had managed to get some more and had given them twenty to thirty, according to their needs. I gave her a little extra. She was a very intelligent sensible woman, with great dignity and a capacity for facing facts. She tells me that most women are expecting an amnesty at Easter—but she doesn't.

Her husband had been a party official for years, a sound and loyal worker. Now he is in prison indefinitely, with no charge against him yet, and so no possibility of getting an advocate. She is allowed to see him once a week for two minutes. All the women go—they have to be there at 7.30 in the morning, and wait in a crowd, standing on the stairs till their names are called. She had a small child, whom she had taken once, but the child had been so frightened and upset that she wasn't going to do it again. And now the child is forgetting her father, and the father is fretting to see the child.

Prison conditions sound pretty bad—great overcrowding, in dirty rooms. Very inadequate sanitary accommodation, and so on. The women are allowed to bring in washing, and money for their husbands to supplement the bad prison food. But none of them have got any extra money to bring now. And, in the two minutes, they can't say much—only she told me she'd tell her husband next time that someone else had come to them from *Ausland*, and he would be glad. And she thanked me for my few pounds, in the name of her town.

It was such a decent, comfortable flat, with radio and piano and books—and now she and the child would have to move into one room. I asked her, too, if anything had been heard of the Dollfuss–Innitzer fund, but she shook her head, and said, " That's only for the families of the Executive "—that's to say, police, soldiers and Heimwehr. I said it was supposed

officially to be for others, but she smiled and shook
her head. She gave me tea, and a friend came in,
who was on the same job of getting names and
distributing. It struck me as being very efficiently
done, much as it would be, say, by English Midland
D.L.P. women.

I asked her about the *Stimmung*—the spirit—here.
But she was very gloomy. All the men were in
prison ; there seemed nothing that they could
reasonably hope for now. Everything was being
systematically crushed. " They want to make all we
have lived for into nothing." I told her the Vienna
rumour that Wiener Neustadt was going Communist. But she said no, many of the young people
were going Nazi, but not Communist. Nor had they
heard anything there of the money from Russia.
She was taking for granted that things were going to
get steadily worse, and she was able to face it. As I
went out, I said, inadequately, that it was a lovely
day. She said yes, and added that *he* had always so
liked the sunshine, that they always went for walks
together in spring. And now she didn't know when
they'd go for walks together again.

She told me, too, of the concentration camp, the
one—or perhaps two—in the town for the Socialists,
and the big one which is being built at Wöllersdorf,
near by, for the Nazis, which will hold 2,500—
rumour has it, with every comfort and convenience !
And she gave me an address to go to in the town, of
a typical case, and there I went next. Still it was

brilliant sunshine ; still there were sweet-smelling bushes, in the park I walked across, with bees coming to them ; still there were birds singing hard into the warmth ; and still I couldn't help enjoying the spring, secretly feeling I had made it myself. And I came to the other address, and a thin and frightened woman let me in.

I couldn't declare myself quite at once, so for a moment I was *Gnädige Frau*, and she looked at me humbly and suspiciously. Then I explained, and she began to tremble, it was so lovely seeing a new friend. And then I was *Genossin* instead of *Gnädige Frau*, and she told me what had happened, how her husband was a gas-worker—they had obviously been doing fairly well ; she had a nice three-roomed flat, and three children. And then, it had all "happened over-night." It had fallen on them. And he was in prison. He has, just yesterday, been moved from the court prison to the *Anhaltelager*, she had no idea for how long—did I believe in the Easter amnesty ?

Remembering the official Legation view, I couldn't say I did much, but I told her about Leoben and Wallisch's grave—as I had told my first friend here. That cheered her up a bit, and she said, "At least it is not as bad here as in Germany." That was what several newspaper correspondents have told me already—only it had rather a different content from her. On the whole, she was probably expecting it to become worse. While I was there, a man from the gas-works, where her husband had

worked, came in, to ask her if she had yet found
another dwelling—hers belongs to the gas-works,
and now they were turning her out. It was in a way
decent of them to have kept her on so long. The
man was quite nice, probably a Nazi—or perhaps
I'm beginning to think that all young men with
square faces and plus-fours are Nazis—and said,
"There'll be an amnesty soon," but neither of
them really believed it. The little girl was listening
all the time. She'd obviously been well fed and looked
after up to now.

What I want to explain, if I can, is that these
people's basic ideas of the universe have been
shattered. And, when an idea is broken, that's
much worse for the people concerned than death or
pain. You see, she believed in justice ; it was an
apparently practical ideal. It was the thing she and
her husband had been working for since they were
young—the basis of their marriage, and of their
bringing children into the world. They had been
good people. And now this had happened. It had
happened to her husband who was a *good* man—
that was what she couldn't understand. She stood
there by her kitchen stove—and it didn't look as if
she had much to cook on it. And she was going to be
turned out of her house, and she had no money, and
she could do nothing. Nothing at all. She had to
stand there with her neck bowed. I don't think I've
ever understood about oppression before. I've
written about it, and imagined it, but here it was.

I suppose I'd always imagined it really from the other side—the men who went on the Krypteia ; I'd always seen it from on top, never from beside. Never the way Glyndwr saw it as a boy in his own home. And, for thousands and thousands of years, men and women have had to stand under the whip, not even answering back. And they've really been people, not a kind of animal, not something different or romantic or picturesque. It's all real. The damned thing's been going on all this time. And now I've seen it, and I will not accept it in my world.

Well, I gave her ten Schillings. First she wouldn't accept it, and then she cried, and just said, " *Genossin, Genossin,*" and held on to me. And the money was damn-all, but the other thing was something. And she whispered to me not to walk to the right, past the sentry ; and then another woman came, and they whispered for a moment, and then we all said, secretly, " *Freundschaft,*" and I went away. In Wiener Neustadt, now, it is like Floridsdorf when I first went there.

In the meantime, Glyndwr had been on to the legal side of things, and came back very depressed. The Socialist lawyers were in prison, mostly, and the one or two who were left were afraid to do anything. The bourgeois lawyers either wouldn't, or were only prepared to work for money—rather a lot of money. He had not been allowed to see the prison.

Things looked altogether pretty grim. Another

story was that some of the employees of the electricity undertaking had found out some bad cases, and collected money for them. The police found this out, confiscated the money, and saw that they lost their jobs. Doctors' names have been taken off the insurance panel lists, so that they lose ninety per cent of their cases, and so on. It is a systematic and capable breaking of the Socialists which is going on. There was curiously little bitterness against the local leaders, all things considered, but that was perhaps loyalty when talking to a foreigner. In general, we got the impression that everyone was terrified, the professionals as well as the workers, and that things were as bad here as the worst we had heard. Of course it *isn't* as bad as Germany, but——

We walked back by the *Anhaltelager*, the concentration camp, an old drill hall, with high windows, out of which no one could look. We wandered round ; there were women standing there—just looking. It was all they could do. Looking and being miserable. I heard two Heimwehr whispering about us—" *Journalisten*." We had both got to the state of anger when one just wants to smack the face of any Heimwehr man. But, after all, if we had, he might have been some wretched unpolitical peasant lad, or even a Socialist who'd had to join to bring five Schillings a week into the family.

Both of us were rather depressed on the journey back to Vienna. And it was my last evening. No immediate job had appeared that we'd got to do at

once, so I changed into my only tidy frock, and we
went out to dinner at the Rathaus Keller, where I
had been last with Dick some nine years ago. It
was just exactly the same. We got a table at the side,
and we had goose-liver with onions, and a thin
Schnitzel, and delicious vegetables, and wine. And
all the waiters kept on hovering round us, not, this
time, to overhear us, but just because we both looked
so happy. It cost us thirteen Schillings, just about
five bob each, which seemed tremendously extrava-
gant—and Glyndwr gave me two red carnations,
one of which I put in my hair. And thirteen Schillings
is as much as some of our fellow Socialists—mother
and children—have to live on for a week. Glyndwr
said : " If you put this in the diary, you'll have the
hell of a time justifying yourself." And yet I don't
feel as if it needed justifying. (I am writing now the
next day.) Nor, I think, does he. He doesn't like me
to say in the diary that at such or such a time he,
as well as I, was happy. He thinks it spoils things,
that it is intellectualising, half living, " here we go
round the prickly pear." But it isn't. It means that
one apprehends things all over, with the mind as
well as the body. But the body's happiness is not
spoilt by the mind watching it. I knew that well,
in the Rathaus Keller, having our party.

We came back then, at once afterwards, I to write,
he to discuss matters with the necessary persons.
Then he brought the bad news. I went on writing
till I was too tired, my eyelids dropping leadenly,

and then I got to bed and waited, hoping he'd come back and tell me what was happening. When he did come, it was to tell me that nothing was altered. All that had happened was that everything had become one degree more dangerous for our friends. But that was only making them laugh and tighten themselves a little against the oncoming of the future. For a few hours I slept heavily, and then woke, as always now, with a start.

MARCH 22ND

All day tidying things up for the end—seeing people ; getting instructions ; trying to get clear in my head what I must above all remember, and what I must on no account omit to forget. Very nice letters from home, tidying up Glyndwr's position ; we were both a lot cheered. There were Heimwehr carrying weapons, and auxiliary of some sort carrying ridiculous but unpleasant little sticks, marching about the streets all afternoon in honour of some Government festivity. One kept on being held up by them.

There was some excitement in the morning, because a plain-clothes man was walking up and down outside. Poor Mr. Q., in spite of everything about him being so extremely above board and excellent, was in a bit of a dither. I felt it would be a bore to be arrested to-day just when I'd got my things packed. But obviously everything's blowing up for a storm, and I *hate* going ! If I hadn't got Denny to meet in Paris, and the meeting to speak at on Sunday, I'd stay. It's like having to catch the last train back to the suburbs before the end of the last act. And I'm really getting to know the trams—and I haven't heard any music yet—and it's a lovely town, *so schön, so schön war es im Roter Wien !* And, of course, it's mostly the people. There's —— and ——, and there's Anne, and there's everyone. Mrs. T. came again ; she was upset, because the Quakers didn't want to have anything to do with her—in spite of her not belonging to any political party ; there are those in the Singer Strasse who, I'm quite sure, would consider her blue eyes and pink cheeks and wavy hair quite unfitting in a relief worker ! And she clung on to me, half crying, and said, " Don't go, don't go ! I have never had a sister before." And, oh, I don't want to go ! And, after I'm gone, I don't know whether I shall ever be able to come back.

I saw S., who confirmed the rumour I'd heard whispered about already—that there are Heimwehr men being brought wounded into Vienna from the west. He thinks it must be some kind of row and mutiny over the disbanding which is going on now. A new law was passed the day before yesterday, forcing every employer to take on one disbanded Heimwehr man to every twenty-five other employees; that will probably mean some kind of dismissal of others. And a law is contemplated by which no firm can get a Government order unless it employs a certain percentage of ex-Heimwehr men. Then I cleared up my accounts, showing how I've spent the money I had from Dick and the others, and my advance royalties. Pretty satisfactory really, both from the political and the humanitarian point of view. I ought to get to England with a credit balance of a few shillings.

Evert had been to a Press lunch to meet Starhemberg—he'd asked me, but I just felt I couldn't— I'm not a good enough journalist for that ! He was a little cross because he'd had to get a clean shirt to go in. And I've never again seen my lady of the leopard-skin coat whom I journeyed out with, but, if she ever reads this, she will understand how it was. And there are all the people I haven't sent picture post-cards to. Oh, well.

I said good-bye to Sam and to Ian, and to everyone, and I wrote bits of diary, and packed. The last job I had to do was another legal report in triplicate, the fastest—and most ill-spelt—piece of typing I've ever done. There wasn't time for dinner after that, only for coffee and cakes at the café where we've met so often. Evert was at his most charming ; we meet again, perhaps, in September. For he's got a big blue passport too, so it's fairly certain that any meeting one plans will not be prevented by at least *that* set of circumstances. Not yet. And Glyndwr I shall see again pretty soon, and, with any luck, we shall work together again, in our own country. But Anne? I wish I knew when I should see her again. I wish I knew for certain that now, now so few hours after I left her, she is still safe and laughing. Not that any of them wouldn't be steady and gay and brave, even if something did happen—even if the plain-clothes men, that we treat as rather a farce, did, after all—— *Verhaftet ; verhaftet*—these damned words.

Anne and her boy-friend, and Glyndwr, came to see me off at the station. Glyndwr and I have amused ourselves making a code, in which we can be, in general, disrespectful to everybody. He hasn't been able, this time, to fulfil his ambition to knock down a Heimwehr man who's knocked me down—anyway, I should rather do my own knocking down—I'm sure I'd be no good at being an inert victim, though I hope I should have the guts to be a completely passive resister, if that were the best thing to be. I kept on wanting something to happen which would force me to stay. All the way to the station I kept on wanting that.

There were a lot of things we might have said to one another on the departure platform, but it was not important, nor even necessary, to say them. We'd got a stage beyond that. Glyndwr kissed me. Then Anne kissed me, and having been so serious, so detailed about serious things, all that morning, we now said silly and loving and feminine things to one another. And then her boy-friend and I kissed one another, and he held me tight for a moment, my cheek to his, whispering, " *Freundschaft* "—there in the crowded, enemy station—and I whispered it back. And then I think we all kissed again, and I got into the train, and the doors slammed all down its sides ; and then we made the other sign, the clenched right fist held not now overhead at proud stretched arm's length for all to see, but secretly, the doubled arm only reaching to shoulder-height. And the last thing I saw was Anne, with the clenched fist hard up to her cheek, and her face white, and her eyes dark and set and wishing me well.

MARCH 23RD

And all night the train was going west across Austria, and I slept uneasily, aware of all I have to do in England, wondering if my carriage companions were friends or enemies, and not able to ask them. And so to Innsbruck in the early morning, and snow mountains and green water, and tufts of wild hepatica in flower under the pines beside the track. I kept on thinking how Glyndwr would have gone wild with pleasure at the snow and sun ; how he'd have hung out of the window to stare. I was worrying a bit about the frontier, only thinking to myself, as it were, in whispers.

And the train went purring on up the Inntal, past the dazzling Arlberg, and down to country less startlingly lovely, and the baby Rhine. And then— we were across the frontier, and nothing had happened. Only another stamp on the blue passport. And the train goes on quite ordinarily towards Paris, so very ordinarily that the whole thing is becoming very difficult to realise. Has it happened ? Is this me ? Was it like that in Vienna, in Leoben ? And if it begins to be hard to believe in already, with the frontier only just passed, what will it be like in England ?

But just as I was writing that, someone came in, and it was Mr. P. Just for a moment, and because he'd come from the other world, I completely failed to recognise him. And then it became immediately plain what was and what wasn't real. There was action to be taken still : practical things to be done, and done immediately. Yes, that was all right. Again I knew where I stood. And as the strangeness, the romance, dried away like dew under sunshine, with the train nearing Paris, so the strong, tough shape of the facts and deductions became more and more apparent.

I am finishing my diary now, but that is just an accident. Whatever was happening while I wrote it,

is happening still. It has all been quite different from
anything I had imagined four weeks ago, less spec-
tacular, less dangerous—for me—far more interesting, far more moving, and with far more moral and
intellectual validity. It has made me more able to
take responsibility, less silly perhaps—at any rate,
less afraid of change and difficulties. Austrian
Socialism is a part of my life as a Socialist now, as
it should be part of the life of all European Socialists,
especially the Socialists of my own country, since we
are in very many ways the same kind of people as
the Austrians, and have the same kinds of problems,
personal, social, and political, to face.

Now, and it may be for another generation or
fifty years, the old savage morality and the old forces
of greed and possession and violence are trying to
kill the new morality and the new idea of brotherhood and equality. Do not let us delude ourselves ;
the old forces still have the power ; they are not any
longer dressed up as kings and barons with gold on
their necks and swords in their hands ; they are
dressed respectably, and their gold is in banks, and
they pay other people to do the killing. And because,
deep down, they have no faith in the future, and
instead of loving mankind they despise and distrust
it, they are becoming more and more vile and brutal.
For cruelty is always caused by fear, and grows with
it. More and more desperately they are trying to
kill the idea of equality and love and freedom, more
and more violently and forcibly they are trying to

crush it out of the minds and spirits of men and women and children. But the future is not with them, or their Churches, or their way of life. The future in Austria is not with Fey and Stahremberg and Dollfuss, nor is it with Mussolini or Hitler. The future in Austria is with the people who believe in the new ideas, whose faith is not shaken by danger or torture or oppression. The future is with the Social Democrats.

To them, from us :

FREUNDSCHAFT UND FREIHEIT.

AFTERWARDS

APRIL 10TH

What follows here is rather important. It seems
likely that anyone reading this diary would suppose
that things in Austria are getting better, that the
need for help is no longer acute—one can stop
fidgeting about Vienna. That is not so. If we care at
all, we have still got to help—still got to show that
brotherhood means something real to us.

Since I came back, I have had news fairly constantly. The Quaker relief work is going on most
efficiently, but within very definite limits. It has
great difficulties, and is always on the verge of inter-
ference by the Dollfuss Government. There are still
quantities of families, both in Vienna and in the
provinces, who are afraid to go to the Quakers, as
they cannot be sure that, in certain eventualities,
their names can be kept from the police. Probably
there are some who have still had no relief at all.

Another side of the picture is that every week
hundreds of men and women are being dismissed,
especially State employees. There was, of course, no
Easter amnesty for the prisoners. Instead, families,
coming back from their Easter week-end in the
country, found that the father had got a notice of

dismissal, on the ground of his being a Socialist or a Jew, or under suspicion of holding some kind of subversive views.

The trials of the Socialist prisoners have begun. The position about legal defence is still extremely unsatisfactory, in spite of the courage of a number of individual lawyers. One of the bravest and most helpful of them has had all his money confiscated. No doubt he is not the only one to whom this kind of thing is happening. I don't know whether he will be able to defend the prisoners whose cases he had taken on ; his title to practise may have gone too. He was thinking very seriously of killing himself.

When we came back from Leoben, three weeks ago, we thought that Paula Wallisch was going to be released, and perhaps allowed to go to her brother and get what peace and healing she could. But there is to be none of that for the widow of Wallisch. Ill and broken as she is, she comes up for trial on the 19th of this month.

My friends in Austria—one or two of whom I wrote in this diary—have been arrested or re-arrested. They are waiting trial now. It is all going on still.

And now : If anyone who has read my diary feels that they would like to let me have any money—whatever amount they can afford—will they send it to me, care of the publishers ? I will see that it gets out to Austria, and the best possible use is made of it. There is still relief work to be done—families whom the Quaker organisation cannot get at. There is still the whole question of legal defence. Anyone who has been reading this diary will understand the kind of things for which money is needed. But if people would rather not send money to me, please let them send it to the Help the Workers of Austria Fund—but to one or the other anyhow !

There is one thing more that I want to write about. On Easter Saturday, Glyndwr and one of the other comrades went to Leoben for the watching of the workers over the grave of Koloman Wallisch. They had brought a wreath of flowers to lay there, from English Socialists. But, when they got to the town, they found everyone afraid and anxious. The pilgrims, who had come there from all over Austria, had been stopped by the police from going to the grave. And the police had taken away all the flowers, and trampled on the grave till it was flat earth. So the people in Leoben whispered to Glyndwr that it was dangerous—he must not go to their grave ; but, all the same, he went, and, as he got near, something happened. The clock struck three, and a Red flag was run up on a tall pine-tree in the wood beside the cemetery. And everyone pointed to it proudly and joyfully, and watched it floating there, the one Red flag flying that day in Austria.

So Glyndwr and his English comrade came into the cemetery of Leoben, and the police rushed at them, and told them they could not see the grave or lay their wreath there, and they did not know what to do. But the sister of Paula Wallisch was by

286

chance in the cemetery too ; they gave the wreath to her, and she, in tears, pleaded with the police officer, and at last she was allowed to lay the English wreath on Wallisch's grave—the only flowers that lay there that day.

They are trying to break and destroy Austrian Socialism. They will not be able to do it. The Red flag will fly again in the pine-woods under the snow mountains. There will be flowers on the graves without crosses—the graves of the hanged leaders whom Dollfuss and his like seek to dishonour. And Socialism will come back in Austria as surely as the spring is coming back in England now.

THE END

LaVergne, TN USA
29 August 2010
195058LV00017B/10/P